BARNS
OF RURAL
BRITAIN

GRAHAM
hughes

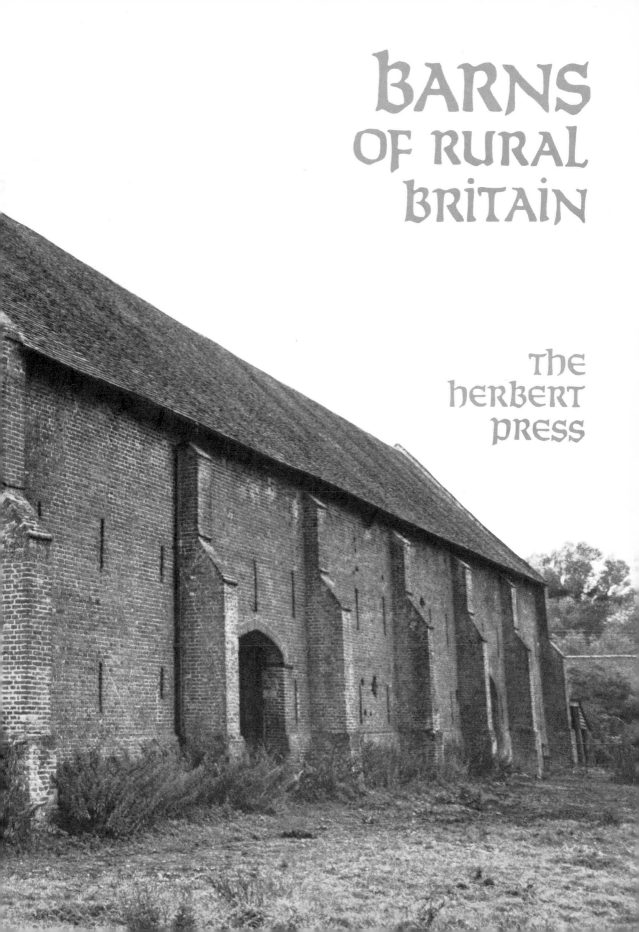

BARNS
OF RURAL
BRITAIN

THE
HERBERT
PRESS

To Serena

Copyright © 1985 Graham Hughes
Copyright under the Berne Convention

First published in Great Britain 1985 by
The Herbert Press Limited, 46 Northchurch Road, London N1 4EJ

Photographs by Graham Hughes, drawings by Richard Reid
Designed by Pauline Harrison

Printed and bound in Great Britain by
BAS Printers Limited, Over Wallop, Hampshire

British Library Cataloguing in Publication Data:

  Barns of rural Britain
  1. Barns—Great Britain—History
  I. Title
  631.2′2′0941   NA8230

ISBN 0 906969 36 0

PREVIOUS PAGE
*One of the great brick barns – the
Gothic style of the buttresses
means an early date. Early 16C.
Old Basing, Hampshire.*

Contents

Preface

Barns were once vital to the economy. Now, they are neglected by almost everyone. Owners have let them decay, developers have demolished them, architects have ignored them, writers and historians have avoided them. Among writers Virginia Woolf is one of the rare exceptions: in her novel *Between the acts* she notes that the great barn in which the refreshments are served 'had been built over seven hundred years ago, and reminded some people of a Greek temple, others of the middle ages, most people of an age before their own'.

There are tens of thousands of barns throughout the country, nostalgic, evocative, sometimes still useful, but usually considered redundant. They were the product of rising prosperity. Over the centuries, wandering nomads became resident farmers; subsistence agriculture became business investment; crops from the country were needed to feed people in the new cities, no longer just the local villagers; improved agriculture increased the abundance of the soil, making large scale storage essential. Barns played their necessary part storing the harvest, providing shelter for threshing during the winter months, often acting as home for the livestock in bad weather. And of course, they were built to store the parson's tithe.

Then came the decline of the barn. The invention of machines for reaping and threshing were the turning point. Cyrus McCormack's first model for a mechanical reaper and harvester made in 1834, now in the Smithsonian Institution in Washington, is a good milestone. His harvest machines won prizes in London's Great Exhibition of 1851. Thereafter the barn as a centre of local industry and wealth, was doomed. Recently, the ever-growing combine-harvesters have become too big and cumbersome to be housed in all but the biggest of the old barns. The cycle of growth and decay is clear, and it has left us to cherish today a wonderful heritage of unspoiled vernacular building.

This is the first book on British barns. I hope it will draw attention to their beauty, to their continuing usefulness, often in new roles after modernization, above all to the need for their preservation. We cannot afford to squander our past. First, we must come to know it; most of the barns seen in this book have never been illustrated before. Then, we must enjoy and use it; I have suggested and described ways in which barns can still serve us. If we don't use them, we will lose them.

OPPOSITE
The wonderful rhythm of equidistant medieval roof bays. Hales, Norfolk, c.1490. No vertical posts — the walls bear the weight of the roof.

ORIGINS
AND USES

The biggest single incentive for building barns was the tithe. Introduced in Anglo-Saxon times, this tithe or tenth of the year's produce had to be paid to the clergy, to help the relief of the poor and the upkeep of the church, and it was stored in a tithe barn often near the church. In the fourteenth century Chaucer praised the good parson who did not 'cursen for his tithes', that is, he did not excommunicate parishioners who did not pay.

Strictly, the name tithe barn means a barn where tithes were stored; it was distinct from the barns or granges (from the medieval *grangia*) where an abbey or monastery would keep its own produce. But because tithes were so important to so many people, the word tithe barn came over the centuries to imply not precise function, but imprecise size. The bigger the barn, the more likely it was to attract the name tithe barn. This verbal evolution has caused much confusion, because the biggest barns (like Abbotsbury in Dorset, for instance) were usually in fact built not for a vicar's tithes, but by a monastic foundation for the purpose of storing its own wealth. It should be called a grange, as at Coggeshall. But it is too late now to try to change the nomenclature of ages: the common use of the words tithe barn at least serves as a reminder that tithes were a dominant motive for the building of medieval barns.

It was not until the enclosure movement of the eighteenth century and the Industrial Revolution of the nineteenth century that the church became less powerful and the tithe system weakened. By the eighteenth century, farmers were using more sophisticated, financial practices: cash payments became customary.

But as late as 1830 in Selborne, in Hampshire, there were serious riots against the high rates of church taxes and tithes. Gilbert White in his diaries of 1789 noted the continual conflict between landowner, tenant and church vestry. This lessened to some extent with the Tithe Commutation Act of 1836, stopping payment of tithes in kind. They were replaced by a rent, payable in cash in January and July, which was based on the average price of corn over a seven-year period. Thus after 1836 many barns which had been used to collect tithes in the form of corn, became redundant and were demolished – one casualty, for example, was the thirteenth-century barn at Ely, 219 feet long, pulled down in 1843. The new system, however, helped to reduce the friction between farmers and clergy.

In 1891 tithes became payable in cash by the landowner instead of by the tenant. After World War I there was a revival of the movement against the payment of tithes. But in some areas, tithes remained a serious burden to village life even as recently as the 1930s. East Anglia, for example, remained predominantly agricultural and residents near Ipswich can remember today the burden of hardship and ill-will which tithes could add to the worries of a poor harvest season. At this time bailiffs were still being sent into the farms to collect the tithe debts, and many farmers were declared bankrupt because they said they could not afford to support the clergy.

There were even seizures – appropriation of the goods and stock of farmers who refused to pay. In the Suffolk village of Elmsett one such farmer lost his farm and stock, and later emigrated to New Zealand. Before he left he recorded the incident in the form of an 8-foot concrete block, taking care first to buy the land on which the memorial was erected. It reads:

1935

TITHE

MEMORIAL

1934

To Commemerate (sic) the Tithe	Herd of Dairy Cows
Seizure at Elmsett Hall	Eight Corn & Seed Stacks
Of Furniture Including	Valued at £1,200 for
Baby's Bed & Blankets	Tithe Valued at £385

In 1925 Parliament stablilized tithes at a fixed charge, and eventually in 1936 abolished them. Today annuities are contributed to but they have dwindled to insignificance and will vanish completely by 1996.

It was only when richer landowners had established themselves that barns as we know them today became necessary. Carlisle Priory, for instance, was founded in the twelfth century. The surrounding country was poor and the neighbouring Scots raided it for whatever surplus they

Barns were usually in the country unless, as here at Carlisle, Cumbria, c.1500, local conditions made necessary the security of being within the medieval city walls.

could find. The tower built in the priory, within the city wall, provided protection for livestock, but the crops were left to the raiders. It was not until the 1490s that local agriculture became prosperous enough, and conditions sufficiently peaceful, to enable Prior Gondibour to build his fine red/sandstone tithe barn, in which to store his pickings from the neighbouring farms.

This increased agricultural prosperity is often explained by the greater power and efficiency of the horse, compared to the ox; over the past thousand years the horse has certainly replaced the ox although oxen were still used on some fields in Sussex as late as 1936.

Barns provided shelter: they had to provide a home for various commodities — normally threshed straw at one end, unthreshed corn at the other, and often hay and livestock too. The doors opened onto the centre of the building, rather than the end, to enable freight to be unloaded easily into the appropriate part of the barn. In areas of exceptional richness like Kent or Essex, a whole barn might be given up to one crop — as at the fine medieval group of barns at Temple Cressing, in Essex, one of the best examples in Europe. Here, one of the huge twelfth/century master/pieces has always been called Wheat Barn, while the other is known as Barley Barn. Each barn is some 150 feet long, so the bulk of the Templars' crops from their neighbouring estate must have been hundreds of cartloads.

A main function for the bigger barns was threshing. In the winter, when threshing was carried out, most barns were the centre of village employment and industry. A flail was used to separate the grain from the chaff and stalks. The thresher swung the handle of the flail over his shoulder and brought down the swingel across the straw just below the ears, so that the grains of corns were shaken out without being bruised. An illustration in the fourteenth/century *Luttrell Psalter* suggests the difficulty of this operation. Skill was needed to handle a flail: it was easier for a novice to hit himself at the back of the neck with the swingel than to get it to fall neatly across the corn. George Messenger, an elderly man from Blaxhall, describes how he first used a flail:

> When I fust used the flail I hit my self such a clout at the back o' the hid! It wholly hurt; the wood was some har! But the ol' boy along o' me said, 'Niver you mind, you'll git one or two of those afore you git used to it. But you'll soon git the swing on it!' And I did, and I used to thrash the corn I growed on my common yard for many years arter that.

While the threshing was going on the big double doors were pinned back, as were the smaller ones in the opposite wall. The through/draught thus set up helped to carry away the chaff and dust. The barn might be orientated so that the prevailing wind would blow through the doors

more effectively. In less windy areas, like Gloucestershire, the doors are often larger. The main doors were large enough for loaded horse-drawn wagons to be driven through; frequently those in the opposite wall, through which the empty wagons left, were lower. A porch was also built where the wagon could shelter from wind and rain while unloading; sometimes, as in Hampshire barns, these porches were enormous, an imposing engineering achievement. There would also be a threshing floor between the doors. If there was no permanent floor the big double doors were sometimes lifted from their hinge pins and laid flat to provide a temporary one. Old wood floors can still be seen in the barn at Folly Farm, Hungerford, and at Lains Barn, Wantage, and fine stone ones at Ablington, Hartpury, Titchfield, and East Riddlesden Hall in West Yorkshire.

The Wheat (left) and Barley (right) Barns of c.1250 and c.1200 at Temple Cressing, Essex, are a great medieval group and still serve a farm of some 700 acres, about the original size.

18C and 19C weatherboarding, huge porch typical of the region. Little Bedwyn, near Marlborough, Wiltshire.

One of the best accounts of the use of a Suffolk barn, comes in the study by G. E. Evans of the country people in the village of Blaxhall near Woodbridge. It was published a generation ago, and is a priceless record of the practice of centuries, now gone for ever. The author describes a typical eighteenth-century Suffolk barn.

The space between the doors was the middlestead of the barn. Here stood the loaded wagon while the corn was stored in the spaces on each side: these were called the goafstead. Here the goaf – or gove – the mow or rich of corn in the straw, was placed ready for threshing. In order to pack as much corn as possible in these two confined spaces, the oldest and there-fore the quietest horse on the farm was used to trample it down as it was unloaded from the wagon. A boy got on the horse's back and rode him round and round treading down the corn. This was known as 'riding the goaf'. As the wagons were unloaded, the corn in the goafstead would mount higher and higher until the boy would find it impossible to ride

OPPOSITE
Stone threshing floor. Ablington, Gloucestershire.

or even lead the horse with any freedom. The horse would then be secured by a long rope expertly fixed around him. The end of the rope was thrown over one of the stout beams of the roof and the men below gently helped the old horse to regain the floor.

The author then describes the flail and how it was made.

The floor of the middlestead was paved with clay-daub – clay beaten down until it became as hard as concrete. The threshing was done with a flail, or a stick-and-a-half as it was called in Suffolk. The half part of the flail was called the swingel, and was made of very tough wood like holly or blackthorn; the handle was made of ash. The handle had a swivel on its top; and the swingel was attached to it by thongs of snake or eel-skin or sometimes just pigskin. The knot was of a special design peculiar to each district. . . . The eel was as much prized for its skin as for its edible qualities; farmers . . . regarded eelskin as the best and toughest leather for tying the swingel of the flail to the handles.

Threshing and dressing (or fyeing) the corn was monotonous, often lonely work. Time passed slowly, and to mark the hours the men cut notches in the side of the barn: the sunlight streaming in oblique winter rays through the doors or a crack in the timbers reached these marks and told them how the day was going and when they could stop for their meals. Threshing was also very tiring, as one Suffolk worker called it, 'real, downright slavery'. Lord Ernle wrote in 1912, ten years after the first self-binder was introduced at Blaxall village, that threshing is 'the most unwholesome of rural occupations'.

Most of the old harvest customs and the old implements went out after the introduction of machinery. Since the arrival of the combine-harvester, much of the corn is not even stacked. But flails went out much later than one would expect. For a long time after the introduction of the threshing machine, a flail was used if the straw was required for thatching. It is likely that the flail was seen last of all – at least serving its ancient purpose – on the common yards or allotments of small cottagers who threshed the wheat they had grown to add to their winter store.

In the old days, before the corn was taken into the barn, the parson would have collected his share of it. One Suffolk local, Henry Puttock, remembers his father telling him what used to happen at the beginning of the nineteenth century. The parson took every tenth sheaf of corn and had his own wagon to cart it to the tithe barn. In some parts of Suffolk the turnips had also to be set in heaps for the parson to tithe.

A few years ago John Goddard, a farmer in the parish of Tunstall, Suffolk, died at the age of ninety-eight; when young, he had to pay a rent of £2 an acre for his farm, plus tithe charges. He recalled that before the introduction of mechanical power he needed thirty horses to work his land:

> When I compare the beginning of my career with the end I realize how amazing the revolution has been. Take one instance – threshing. At one time the farmer did not go to the stack: the stack, in a manner of speaking, was brought into the barn. I remember them using the stick-and-a-half in the barns to beat out the corn from the straw; and they had been using that since the days of the Bible. They had fans, too, to get rid of the chobs, the chaff as they call it now; they tried all sorts of contrivances to separate the chaff from the corn. But today there's little talk of barns: with the combine-harvester they've even done away with the stacks!

As outdoor mechanical threshing replaced indoor hand threshing, so the stackyard replaced the barn. The stack was thatched to keep the rain out and left relatively loose, to allow some air circulation to dry the straw. Plastic sheeting has now replaced thatch, and the tractor has made even the stackyard obsolete. Bales of trussed straw may be found anywhere, compact, tight and easy to move. The barn is no longer essential to store crops.

As well as the harvest the barn might also house livestock. The animals would trample on the dry straw and transform it with dung into fertile spring manure. Cattle stabled below the stored produce would provide warmth to dry it. Thus cattle and livestock would help the barn give the best and fullest use to its owner. Multi-purpose barns were more common in the poorer areas of the country – for example, the Devonshire long house accommodated people, cattle and corn, each in their own allotted portion.

Typical Devon long house, once housed five families with livestock. Its use included that of a traditional barn, but was much more diverse. Chapple Farm, Gidleigh, Devon.

Bank barns in the north were built on a slope with two storeys one end : fodder was easily pushed from the upper storey to the animals below. A rare medieval field bank barn at Kilnsey, North Yorkshire.

Red sandstone columns beneath granary give massive effect. Llangarron, near Ross-on-Wye, Hereford and Worcester.

Sometimes in barns there was a space below the threshing floor for animals – the bank barns and field barns in the Lake District and in Yorkshire were built so that fodder could be tipped from the upper gallery to the cattle below. This practice provided maximum efficiency with minimum effort and was possible because the barn was built on a steep slope; the crops could be unloaded at ground level on one side, while cattle could walk in also at ground level on the lower side.

Very often, especially in the south, cattle sheds formed part of an enclosed or partly enclosed yard, bounded at right angles by the barn, and sometimes built into the barn timbers. This arrangement of sheds or hovels, as they were called in the southeast, was the product not of early poverty but of the increased prosperity of the bigger farms in the eighteenth and nineteenth centuries.

Many barns combined the functions of cattle shed, wagon shed, barn, granary and dovecot, as at the Llangarron complex in Hereford and Worcester or Southrop near Cirencester in Gloucestershire. Pigeons had three admirable aspects: they produced delicious eggs, they made fine guano manure, and, when winter meat tended to be scrawny because of lack of sustenance for livestock, they were eaten after being trapped in their one-ended nesting boxes. The dovecot was therefore extremely useful, very often being built into the wall of the barn as at Kelmscott Manor in Oxfordshire or West Pennard in Somerset. A fine detached square

Medieval dovecot in the outshot porch. The kneelers at the bottom of the eaves are unusually ornate. Wesley preached inside. Grassington, North Yorkshire.

dovecot dated 1656 survives in a field on the model estate at Hodnet in Shropshire.

Storage had to be in a convenient place and barns are always found either near the farmyard and farmhouse, where the workers could gain easy access, or in the open country at the centre of a group of fields, where some form of intermediate storage was necessary before the produce was used or sent to market. It is the latter type of country barn which is in great danger today. Thus, for example, in one small 10-mile area of Sussex farmland, a dozen large old country barns have recently collapsed and vanished near Folkington, Winton Street, Alfriston, Berwick and Bishopstone. These isolated barns were close to the crops but difficult to reach from the roads, and now are seldom wanted by the local farmer – when fast mechanized communications are vital.

Dovecots were a vital source of winter food; they were often built near barns or sometimes, as here, combined. West Pennard, Somerset, c.1400. National Trust.

OPPOSITE
Farm buildings were seldom so elaborate as this dovecot of 1656 at Hodnet, Shropshire.

Architecturally, a big change came with the introduction of the Dutch barn, built with one side, and sometimes one end or both, supported on columns, and open to the weather, for easy loading of the ever-increasing harvest bulk. The Dutch seem to have been first with the idea that a barn for storing hay simply does not need walls; they built a sort of tiled umbrella, supported on a wooden pole with pegs and peg holes in it to allow the roof height to be adjusted according to the bulk of harvest to be contained. These economical huts can be seen as early as the sixteenth century in the pictures of, for instance, Breughel. The 'Dutch barn', usually with two or three walls, reached Britain from the seventeenth century.

An early Dutch barn used for storing hay, perhaps c.1700, easy for manoeuvre and storage, bad for threshing and shelter. East Lambrook, Somerset.

They were especially well-adapted for storing hay. An early example, perhaps around 1700, is the barn at East Lambrook in Somerset, while a recent one of the 1930s can be found at Tremedda in Cornwall, and a fine-quality brick giant at Welbeck Abbey in Nottinghamshire, typical of many built around 1800. But most Dutch barns post-date the arrival of mechanical threshing. They were good for storing hay or straw, bad for open-air threshing, as the through-draught could not be controlled, and there was no porch to shelter the wagons. The Dutch barn heralded the Agricultural Revolution: it indicates storage of the finished product instead of shelter to carry out the preparatory work which was now to be done in the fields.

Gilbert White of Selborne gives a fair idea of the importance of barns and of the large numbers of farmworkers who might be involved on a special village project:

April 26 1766: Finished moving my barn, which I set at the upper end of the orchard. It began to move on Thursday the 17, and went with great ease by the assistance of about 8 men for that little way that it went in a straight line: but in general it moved in a curve, and was turned once quite round, and left way round again. When it came to the pitch of the hill it required 20 hands; and particularly when it wanted to be shoved into its place wideways, parallel with the Collins's hedge.

Near one day of the time was taken up in making new sills, one of which was broken in two by the screwing it round sideways. No accident happened to the workmen, or labourers, and no part of the framework was broken or dislocated, so as to do any material damage.

The workmen were 3 days in pulling down ye skillings, and blocking and removing obstructions, previous to ye removal. The barn is 40 feet long. August 20 1774: Vast dew, sweet day. On this day Farmer Spencer built a large wheat rick near his house, the contents of which all came from a field near West⁄croft barn, at the full distance of a mile. Five wagons were going all day.

A hundred years later, barns were still central to rural life in remote Dorset. In *The Mayor of Casterbridge* (1886) one of the climactic moments is the violent wrestling fight between Henchard and Farfrae. It is no coincidence that Hardy placed this wonderful scene not in a home or a market place but in the building which meant most to both men, and indeed to the whole farming community, the grain barn.

Cobbett in his *Rural Rides* of 1823 notes angrily of the corn country on the Isle of Thanet in Kent:

All was corn around me. Barns, I should think, two hundred feet long: ricks of enormous size and most numerous . . . The people dirty, poor⁄looking; ragged, but particularly dirty . . . Invariably have I observed, that the richer the soil, and the more destitute of woods, that is to say, the more purely a corn country, the more miserable the labourers. The cause is this, the great, the big bull frog grasps all. In this beautiful island, every inch of land is appropriated by the rich.

Burns had also noted forty years before that better land led to worse conditions for the worker. It was the landlord or bull frog who profited. George Crabbe reflected the same envy two hundred years ago: 'Our farmers round, well pleased with constant gain, like other farmers, flourish and complain.' George Eliot makes a similar point in *Middlemarch* of 1871:

The mossy patch of the cowshed, the broken grey barn⁄doors, the pauper labourers in ragged breeches who had nearly finished unloading a waggon of corn into the barn ready for early thrashing.

The impact of picturesque, romantic decay on barns is not so new as some theorists believe. Emily Brontë may have used Top Withens Farm⁄house and farm settlement as her model for *Wuthering Heights* (1847). Now in decay, this romantic group is a 3⁄mile walk along a rough track over the moors from Haworth, a reminder that barns served agriculture which was often remote and inaccessible.

Hardy's *Far From The Madding Crowd* (1874) shows that barns were used for sheep as well as for corn:

They sheared in the Great Barn, called for the nonce the Shearing⁄barn, which on ground⁄plan resembled a church with transepts. It not only emulated the form of the neighbouring church of the parish but vied with it in antiquity . . . The dusky filmed, chestnut roof, braced and tied by huge collars, curves and diagonals, was far nobler in design, because more wealthy in material, than nine-tenths of those in our modern churches.

Today the large side doors were thrown open towards the sun to admit a bountiful light to the immediate spot of the shearers' operations, which was a wooden threshing-floor in the centre, formed of thick oak, black with age and polished by the beating of flails for many generations, till it had grown as slippery and as rich in hue as the stateroom floors of an Elizabethan mansion. Here the shearers knelt, the sun slanting in upon their bleached shirts, tanned arms, and the polished shears as they flourished, causing them to bristle with a thousand rays strong enough to blind a weak-eyed man. Beneath them the captive sheep lay panting, quickening its pants as misgiving merged in terror, till it quivered like the hot landscape outside . . . So the barn was natural to the shearers, and the shearers were in Harmony with the barn.

One essential component of the scene has been so far omitted, and who better to introduce it than the national poet of Scotland, Robert Burns. He wrote, 'I have not the most distant pretensions to being what the guardians of the escutchions call a Gentleman. I am simply Robert Burns

Typical of thousands of decaying barns. This one was unusual and lucky; it was repaired in 1980 by its owner farmer. West Meon, Hampshire.

at your service. I was born to the plough.' The plough was once his symbol and his hope, and the symbol of the efficiency of the plough lies in the barn where it and its produce were stored. The mouldboard plough may have been invented in Denmark a thousand year ago. Its increasing use since then led to ever increasing productivity from the soil. The size and quality of the barns that were built reflect to some extent the prosperity of a region's agriculture. The Scottish borders, Burns' homeland, have few barns, because as Burns himself discovered, farming there is difficult. His family farm, typical of his region, was seldom productive or profitable, even when he became a tenant farmer in his own right after his father's death in 1784.

More recently, Virginia Woolf gives two retrospective salutes to Sussex barns today lying neglected and alone, in her masterpiece *The Waves* (1931): 'Barns and summer days in the country, rooms where we sat all now lie in the unreal world which is gone . . . To be loved by Susan would be to be impaled by a bird's sharp beak, to be nailed to a barnyard door . . .' Birds' carcases were nailed to barn doors in the hope of deterring other birds from eating the grain inside.

Perhaps the barn was once the mose useful building in England. Today it is certainly the most neglected.

THE AGRICULTURAL REVOLUTION

PREVIOUS PAGE
Another crisp northern building, probably designed by John Carr of York c.1795, now redundant for agriculture. Turner lived and painted next door. Farnley, near Otley, West Yorkshire.

by the mid-eighteenth century the idea of labour-saving was born. Already by 1770 the Secretary of the Royal Society of Arts had invented a dynamometer to measure the pulling power of different types of horse and harness. However low the cost of labour might be, efficiency was now seen to have a scientific value of its own.

The ox-yolk had been succeeded over the centuries by improved horse-collars and harnesses, to which were added the fruits of the Industrial Revolution: the iron horseshoe, the deep plough and the horse-drawn drill. In about 1730 Jethro Tull devised his machine to plant seeds in rows. The self-sharpening iron plough-share, introduced around 1770 by Robert Ransome, the Quaker brass-founder, fortified the plough and made it more efficient and long lasting. The share was made with metal of graded hard-ness, so that the soft portion wore away in use, leaving an ever-sharp point. In 1789 the all-iron plough was introduced.

In 1784 Andrew Meikle, an old Dunbar millwright, invented a mach-ine flail for separating grain from straw; it was patented in 1788. This machine for threshing was still horsedrawn: it was placed in the barn

Main sources of barn wealth at the medieval barn, South Stoke, Avon; horse engine-house or gin c.1800; threshing porch; and dovecot c.1300.

while the horses provided the power outside. Three or four horses in the open air would pull round a big pole attached to what was called in Yorkshire a ginny wheel. A ramp would help the horses over the gear shaft which went through a hole in the barn wall and could be attached to the various machines inside. At West End near Blubberhouses in North Yorkshire, this 'sweep' method was still common as late as 1932, the machines being used for threshing, winnowing, chopping, and for pulping mangles. A more sophisticated crown wheel and pinion gear driving an overhead horizontal drive shaft was an expensive alternative; the horses and their circular route would then be housed in a purpose-built round or many-sided shed on one side of the barn, towards the end. One, for drawing water, is still standing at Stanmer Park, Brighton. Some farms like Cutsey, at Trull in Somerset, were built in the 1860s incorporating a steam engine in their design, although in England the steam engine and travelling threshing box were usually hired from a specialized contractor; their arrival brought delight to the children but doom to the cart horse. The mass production tractor of the 1930s and the combine-harvester

Granite horse-gin c.1800.
Titchberry, Cornwall. National
Trust.

of the 1950s completed the development of the instant harvest; what in the Middle Ages took a year and hundreds of people to complete, now takes a week and a machine. In 1850 over one-quarter of British men worked in agriculture. By 1911 the number was less than one in eleven. In 1961 the total had dwindled to one in eighteen and the decline still continues sharply. The modern farm is mechanized.

Old barns often have doors too small for the giant modern machines to enter, columns too close for the machines to turn inside, windows too small to illuminate the work, roofs too low for the height of the harvester machine. So the barn for threshing is often thought to be redundant. New barns are rarely graceful but they are spacious and versatile. Grain is stored in circular silos or bins, hay is baled mechanically and stacked in the field where the cattle need it. Straw is often buried in dykes, ready to be turned into spring manure.

Agriculture slowly became fashionable; the gentleman farmer appeared on the scene. Thomas Coke of Holkham Hall in Norfolk was a great agricultural innovator who claimed to have spent half a million pounds on new farm buildings. Recent researches have shown how seriously he related aesthetics to productivity on his model farmsteads. For the first time some farm buildings were designed by architects instead of masons and carpenters; the Great Barn at Holkham (by Wyatt *c.*1790) is typical with its clear lines so different from the softer outlines of the Middle Ages.

OPPOSITE ABOVE
New barns, even when they are
well-designed as here, do not
harmonize with the old (nor with
the countryside). It is visually
better and often financially cheaper,
to keep and adapt the old.
Tregarthen, near Zennor,
Cornwall.

OPPOSITE BELOW
One of Lord Anson's model 18C
farm buildings at Shugborough,
Staffordshire, which housed
Britain's first stationary threshing
machine.

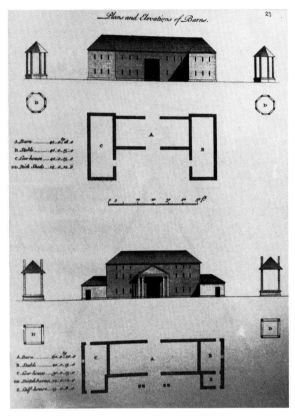

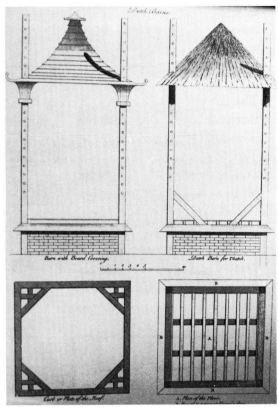

The involvement of Lord Anson (Coke's son-in-law) at Shugborough was only marginally more modest. Some experts disapproved of this dilettante interest, not realizing their own 'expert' opinions might conceal a stuffy aversion to experiment and change. For instance, in 1812 H. E. Strickland wrote in his *General View of the Agriculture of the East Riding of Yorkshire* for the Board of Agriculture:

But the folly even of an overbuilt farmhouse is surpassed by that of an ornamental one. What, indeed, can be so absurd and devoid of taste as a Gothicised farmhouse, or Castellated cottage? To the credit, however, of the landowners of this country, such incongruities seldom occur.

Arthur Young, indefatigable traveller and recorder of the unmemorable, gave advice in his *Farmer's Calendar* in 1804:

The fashionable sheep-shearings, farming clubs, societies, etc., render another remark not absolutely unnecesssary: a steady careful old farmer may not be the worse for mixing a good deal in the company of much higher rank than his own; but a young man with a small degree of animation may suffer by it. His eye and his mind become insensibly accustomed to objects and habits of living to which he was before a stranger. If after an excursion which has carried him into great, and what is called good company, he returns home not quite so well satisfied with home as he was before, he has contracted a taint that may be worse than the scab among his sheep.

The advance towards agricultural industry often began where mining or factory activities already existed, to provide winter employment which elsewhere would depend upon threshing: the phasing out of the winter employment in the barns everywhere was a slow and painful process, just as it was remorseless.

In the United States in the mid-1830s, Obed Hussey of Cincinnati and Cyrus McCormick of West Virginia, each invented a mechanized reaper. McCormick opened a factory to manufacture his invention in Chicago in 1847, fascinating Britain with his display at the Great Exhibition of 1851. Hiram Pitts of Maine invented a threshing machine in 1837, launching it in Europe at the Paris Exhibition of 1855; it could thresh 740 litres of wheat in an hour compared with the 36 litres claimed by six men in the same period. By 1861 the first threshing machine was working in South Australia, again to the immediate detriment of the workers but the long-term financial benefit of the farmers. British engineers designed steam engines for farm work in the 1880s. The oil-powered tractor appeared

One of Britain's grandest barn groups, built at Tixall, Staffordshire, to fill all the needs of the Agricultural Revolution, mid-19C.

in the Mid-West in the United States in 1889. Primitive combine-harvesters, drawn by up to forty horses or mules, were used in California and the Mid-West before 1900. The population of England and Wales rose from 12 million in 1821 to 26 million in 1881, a rapidly growing market for the farmers. But cheap American grain reversed the trend towards agricultural prosperity at home. The prairies and the new American mechanization produced the corn: reliable steamships for the first time could bring American produce to England easily. From 1860 to 1890, the price of corn in Britain was halved.

The reason for the increase in poverty was the rise in population rather than the expropriation of small farms. There were more families employed on the land in 1831 than in 1801 (761,000 compared with 697,000), but hardship there was, and in places very severe. During the Napoleonic Wars, prices rose steeply, while farm labourers' wages remained at a standstill. Legislation to keep the price of corn at artificially high levels after the peace of 1815 hardly mitigated the effects of the introduction of the threshing machine. Subsequent low prices and a labour surplus had dire results: in 1830 riots throughout the countryside were partly promoted by the mysterious 'Captain Swing' who signed and circulated many blood-chilling letters.

In East Sussex, Chyngton Barn in Seaford was burned down in 1835 by farmworkers protesting at their low pay and poor working conditions. In Norfolk, a broadsheet was printed at Fakenham, declaring:

We the undersigned Magistrates acting in and for the Hundred of Gallow, in the County of Norfolk, Do promise to use our utmost Endeavours and Influence we may possess, to prevail upon the Occupiers of Land in the said Hundred, to discontinue the use of Threshing Machine and to take them to pieces. Dated this 29th day of November, 1830. Chas Townshend, Robert Norris, Edw. Marsham.

Strikes and protests were increasingly common: labourers like the Chartists of 1848 saw their agricultural jobs threatened by the new agricultural machinery.

They wanted to 'live to see the restoration of old English times, old English fare, old English holidays and old English justice, and every man live by the sweat of his brow.' The Anti-Corn Law League nevertheless lobbied successfully for free trade, which meant larger-scale agriculture and more machines.

Barn museum complexes showing these 'old times' can be visited at:

Acton Scott in Shropshire – a working farm designed to bring town dwellers into the real countryside.
Avebury in Wiltshire.

ABOVE
*Barn recently restored as an
agricultural museum, mostly by
local voluntary contributions.
Avebury, Wiltshire.*

LEFT
Inside the Avebury museum

35

Avoncroft Museum of Buildings, Bromsgrove, Hereford and Worcester.

Banks Barn, Banks, near Brampton, Cumbria.

Breamore, near Fordingbridge in Hampshire – the feudal village preserved by Sir Edmund Hulse includes a barn with an agricultural museum 200 yards away.

Chiltern Open Air Museum, at Chalfont St Giles in Buckinghamshire – a cruck-frame barn here measures 42 feet by 18 feet, a type common in the Midlands but rare in the southeast. It was moved from Arborfield near Reading in 1980, rethatched and given new woven wattle walling, as a gift from the National Institute for Research into Dairying.

Michelham in East Sussex – some good Sussex farm wagons.

Norton's Farm, Sedlescombe, near Battle, East Sussex – a plough from 1860 and wagons.

Old Burlesdon, Hungerford Bottom, Hampshire. Agricultural bygones.

The Somerset Rural Life Museum, Abbey Farm, Glastonbury, Somerset – agricultural implements in the Abbey Barn.

Upminster, Greater London.

The Weald and Downland Open Air Museum, Singleton, near Chichester, West Sussex – good examples of vernacular architecture.

Whiston, South Yorkshire – a museum of rural life is planned for the Long Barn here.

Wilmington Priory, East Sussex – exhibits implements (the main barn burned down thirty years ago).

Wye College Agricultural Museum, Brook, Kent. Fine barn c.1374 exhibiting all sorts of implements.

There is a special feast for the barn lover in East Sussex: small but choice, it is called Exceat. Cleaned but barely changed from its eighteenth-century form by its sensitive architect, Wycliffe Stutchbury, this barn is now the headquarters of the Seven Sisters Country Park set up by the East Sussex County Council in 1971 helped by a government grant. Built in c.1750, it is a typical Sussex construction with bays, principal posts forming an aisle down one side, jowls to support the roof trusses, and tie beam and two small diagonal queen posts or struts above. Being on a slope the barn has an unusual two-level floor. It has continually changing exhibitions of local farming and nature, what might be called barn technology, and to complement this 'teaching' barn, it even has an accompanying 'working' barn with cobwebs and bales of straw for children to sit on while learning about the country.

On Scotland's Tayside the Angus Folk Museum at Glamis covers both the diminutive Scottish barns, their work and their contents – the thravers, caff, luggies, theek, hingin lums, and perley pigs: the vocabulary is as good as the display.

The most notable folk-life museum north of the border – the Auchindrain Museum of Country Life is near Inveraray, Strathclyde.

Home of the Seven Sisters
Country Park at Exceat, East
Sussex.

Collections of the old tools which lessened the toil of the peasant —
the ploughs and spades and forks, the harrows and harnesses, the adzes
and axes and saws, the buckets and barrels and measures — are on display
in museums at Newbury, at Bibury where David Verey, the distinguished
art historian, was a devoted enthusiast, at Amberley Castle in West Sussex
whose Chalkpit is a unique spectacle, and elsewhere. The Athelstan
Museum in Malmesbury, Wiltshire, has two shovels used for tossing grain.

At Newton, near Stocksfield, Northumberland is the Hunday National
Tractor and Farm Museum, started in 1955 by John Moffitt. Situated
in buildings dating from 1806, important in themselves, it includes a
circular Northumberland wheel-house or 'gin gang' of the mid-nineteenth
century. Within the museum are some two hundred early agricultural
machines which led to the development of the combine-harvester and
resulted in the demise of the barn.

Other museums illustrating the development of agriculture and barns
are found at:

Castle Farm, Marshfield, Avon.
The Cotswold Folk Museum at Burford, Gloucestershire.

The Dorset County Museum, Dorchester, Dorset.

The James Countryside Museum, Bicton Gardens, East Budleigh, Devon.

The Museum of East Anglian Life, Stowmarket, Suffolk.

Museum of English Rural Life, University of Reading, Reading, Berkshire.

Norfolk Rural Life Museum, Gressenhall, Norfolk.

North of England Open Air Museum, Beamish Hall, Beamish, Stanley, Co. Durham.

Oxfordshire County Museum, Fletcher's House, Woodstock, Oxfordshire.

Priest House Country-life Museum, Brympton d'Evercy, Yeovil, Somerset.

Rutland County Museum, Catmose Street, Oakham, Leicestershire.

Ryedale Folk Museum, Hutton-le-Hole, North Yorkshire.

Shugborough Park, Staffordshire. Lord Anson's model farm *c.*1800 with several buildings illustrating agricultural history.

Welsh Folk Museum, St Fagans, Cardiff, South Glamorgan.

West Yorkshire Folk Museum, Shibden Hall, Halifax, West Yorkshire.

Weyhill Wildlife Park and Rural Life Museum, Weyhill, Andover, Hampshire.

The White House Country Life Museum, Aston Munslow, Shropshire.

CONSTRUCTION

PREVIOUS PAGE
*Superb 13C roof shelters many
functions beneath. Boxley, Kent.*

*Line drawings showing types of construction, joints etc. can be found in the glossary
at the end of the book.*

There are three main types of barn building. First is the box or
basilica, where the walls are the structure: there are no internal
vertical load-bearing supports. Good examples built in brick are
at Old Basing in Hampshire and Copdock in Suffolk; in stone, there
is Buckland in Devon; in flint, Patcham in East Sussex; and in timber,
a myriad of smaller barns throughout the country. Beautiful decorations
are formed by the brick in-fills in the timber frames forming the walls
at Hodnet, near Market Drayton in Shropshire; in the Earl of Leicester's
barn at Kenilworth in Warwickshire; and in the similar tithe barn at
Thame in Oxfordshire, all built in the sixteenth century.

The second type of barn construction, used from the twelfth century
until the nineteenth century, is the post and truss. Here, it is the internal
frame, not the external walls, which takes the roof weight. The posts meet
and support the roof timbers, or tie beams, which in turn hold up the
roof itself. Sometimes, as at Great Coxwell or at Bolton Abbey, Yorkshire,
a wooden skeleton supports a stone shell, but often the outer shell is timber
like the beams within.

The third type of construction is the cruck frame: this is a series of
large paired timbers — at Leigh Court, Hereford and Worcester, they are

*An early 16C brick masterpiece
with crow-stepped gables.
Copdock, near Ipswich, Suffolk.*

ABOVE
Brick nogging in-fills were popular in Tudor times, and were the commonest early use of brick. Hodnet, 1619, Shropshire. Other similar big brick barns are at Thame and Kenilworth.

LEFT
A box-frame barn, c.1600, whose timber was intended to be shown as decoration, not plastered over. Izaak Walton lived next door. Near Stafford, Staffordshire.

Box-framed barn, c.1600, with the wood deliberately used as decoration. Salford, near Chipping Norton, Oxfordshire.

Typical medieval post and truss barn construction. The posts, not the walls, take the roof weight. Alciston, East Sussex.

each about 36 feet long – erected as a series of inverted Vs. These crucks bear the load of the roof, and they make possible a considerable internal width – Leigh is about 34 feet wide. Usually, the halves of a cruck were carved from one big tree – often oak.

The two main species of oak are the Sessile Oak and the Pedunculate Oak. The first has small branches, normally too small for crucks, and its acorn grows in its cup seated on the branch. The second sort of oak has a much broader sweep to its shape, including long curved branches which could be divided down the middle to form a pair of cruck blades. Its acorn has a small stalk or peduncle, hence the common name. The distribution of these species determined to some extent the location of cruck-framed buildings.

The cruck was widespread throughout much of the Midlands and the southwest, but it was most common in Wales and the western half of England spreading even up to Scotland in the area round Stirling. Aisled

One of the grandest medieval roof structures showing the huge scale of early medieval timbers used in post and truss construction. Great Coxwell, near Faringdon, Oxfordshire. 13C. National Trust.

LEFT
Big doors, like these 18C doors in the medieval transept here (left) were often a later addition probably needed to accommodate the larger wagons bearing the abundant harvest of improved agriculture. Great Coxwell, near Faringdon, Oxfordshire.

BELOW LEFT
Monastic barns were usually very large. Bolton Abbey, North Yorkshire, probably c.1300, with 18C restorations.

Medieval cruck blades, Leigh, near Worcester, Hereford and Worcester.

The exterior of the barn at Leigh, Hereford and Worcester.

post and truss barns proliferate in the south and east, from Portland Bill to the Fens. These two types of barn construction overlap widely, particularly in Hampshire, the Thames Valley and the Chilterns.

The internal timbers may be a half or a quarter section of a tree. They are usually arranged with the soft sapwood (the outer layer of the tree) facing towards the outside wall of the barn, the hard heartwood (the central portion of the tree) facing inwards. This fairly common habit is probably practical rather than artistic: sapwood rots more quickly and is attacked by furniture beetles, whereas the oak heartwood is almost imperishable, and was therefore placed where it was structurally most necessary.

Prefabrication was the rule from very early times. The weight of the bigger timbers was enormous and the value of the unused wood considerable. For these reasons a timber-frame construction was prepared in the forest where the trees were cut. Each piece of wood was jointed into its neighbour, numbered, carried to the building site and reassembled there. The Roman numerals giving the key to the position are a common feature of many old roofs: for instance in the barns at Boxley in Kent (thirteenth-century), Egstow in Derbyshire (fourteenth-century), Hilders, Bough Beech in Kent (sixteenth-century), Duke's Green, Alfriston in East Sussex (seventeenth-century), and at Horam in East Sussex (eighteenth-century).

After the Reformation, the size of individual timbers in barns steadily decreased. Vertical posts became shorter and thinner, and floor rafters narrower. Whatever the reason, the biggest timbers, as at Great Coxwell, are usually thirteenth of fourteenth century. The lessening in size over the centuries was so noticeable that the fattening at the top of the wood columns, called the jowl, slowly vanished to be replaced by a triangular block of wood called a knee, fixed to the top of the post. Hardwood was so valuable that the whole tree was used: sapwood as well as heartwood, perhaps to get the maximum benefit from the large, slow growth. Big timbers were often reused. Carpenters' numbers at the end of the beams guided the order of assembly. If the carpenters' numbers no longer coincide, as at Dean's Water Mill Barn, Lindfield, West Sussex, there is a presumption of reuse. Reuse was especially common round the coast, where wrecking and smuggling, or simply the purchase of old timbers from the breakers' yards, made ships' timbers available for barns. The navy needed oak, and therefore (from the eighteenth century) controlled its supply, further aggravating the scarcity for barn-building purposes.

Reuse of stone is sometimes easier to trace than reuse of timber: the sixteenth-century barn at Burrow Hill Farm near One Tree Hill in Somerset has ferocious lions jumping from its walls, but they have not always been imprisoned there: they began life in the fourteenth century at Muchelney Abbey but must have been removed when the walls were partly demolished at the Dissolution. Selborne village in Hampshire has

Medieval cruck blade at Pirton, Hereford and Worcester.

Early roof beams were prepared near the forest to minimize the bulk to be transported. They were then assembled on site in accordance with the carpenters' marks. Hilders Farm, Bough Beech, Kent.

Adze marks and irregularity in some humble country barns suggest how laborious the shaping of timber beams was before modern tools became available, as here at Alkington Manor, Shropshire. Grander medieval barns, however, show impeccable wood work.

As good timber became scarcer, the swelling at the top of the post, called a jowl, became sharper and less strong, as here at Horam, East Sussex, c.1753.

many Gothic details taken from its abbey buildings. Manor Farm at Twyford, Hampshire has used stones from the monastic grange once on the site; a main post in the seventeenth-century barn here has an incongruous, inverted Romanesque capital as its plinth. At Stoke in north Devon the opposite, and equally common process, is found: the medieval buttresses and plinths of the barn belonging to nearby Hartland Abbey have almost been submerged beneath modern, practical additions. At West Acre in Norfolk, eighteenth-century roof and doors have been fitted to the medieval structure.

Most outside wood cladding is relatively new. Horizontal weatherboarding seems to have existed in the early sixteenth century, to judge from surviving examples on dwellings, and from early references to building methods. But weather-boarding requires planks of a constant thickness, and consistency in carpentry is achieved by using good saws. A fourteenth-century drawing in the British Museum in London shows a log leaning with one end on a trestle; the top sawyer, who guided the saw, stands on the log and the bottom sawyer, who pulled it, stands underneath. Thin planking of modern aspect could hardly result from such an imprecise emplacement. Saw pits dug in a carefully drained sloping pitch of ground, are mentioned as early as the sixteenth century, and so are saw-mills powered by wind and water, though these did not become common in the south until the late eighteenth and the nineteenth centuries.

Cleaving with axe and wedge, then squaring up with an adze was the alternative method to sawing, resulting in the rough and wavy scantling so common and so appealing in big medieval beams. Up to the seventeenth

A solid brace between vertical and horizontal was called a knee; 15C gatehouse barn hall at Mavesyn Ridware, Staffordshire.

Medieval lion still in the wall of Muchelney Abbey, Somerset, which was partly demolished during the Reformation in 16C when some of the masonry was reused elsewhere.

Medieval walls often have newer roofs and doors, here 18C, at West Acre, Norfolk.

century, cleaving was a standard method for producing 'clapboard', made from logs split into wedge-shaped planks, radially from the centre. Cleft timber is more durable than sawn because the surface follows the grain and is therefore less likely to split. But successful cleaving depends upon the availability of good timber with straight grain and no knots.

Probably cleaving gave way to pit sawing for the production of planks in the eighteenth century when saws, both hand and power-driven, became more efficient. From then on, feathered-edged or weather-boarding walls, with thin horizontal planks, must have become very cheap and easy to build.

A report by Charles Vancouver on Hampshire to the Board of Agriculture in 1813 — one of many such regional surveys which today give a vivid insight into the countryside of the time — lists some typical costs:

Sawing and hewing, per hundred feet oak, ash, elm, beech and poplar under 18 inches in width of board, from 3/6d. to 4/- per 100 feet . . . the cost of sawn elm boards $\frac{3}{4}$ inch thick, 4d. per square foot, beech and other weather-boarding, $\frac{3}{4}$ inch from 12/- to 18/- per 100 feet . . . Common five-barred gates from 12/- to 18/- each.

The earlier barns probably had vertical plank cladding, as may be seen today in the original portion of the exterior of the barns at Frindsbury

Medieval exterior wood cladding is now extremely rare, but seems usually to have been in vertical strips, not, as more recently, horizontal. Horizontal weatherboarding is probably only effective with the use of efficient modern saws to prepare regular planks. Harmondsworth, Greater London.

The finest medieval barn interior in Kent, at Frindsbury, with modest exterior.

in Kent (*c.*1300), at Upminster in Essex (*c.*1430), or at Harmondsworth in Greater London (*c.*1400).

The name 'midstrey' suggests a mid-way opening rather than two or three distributed throughout the length of a barn; one opening was more usual in medieval Kent as in the barns at Frindsbury or Littlebourne. It seems, too, that the biggest porches, like repeated entrances, were a later invention – the big doors of medieval Great Coxwell, Oxfordshire, are eighteenth-century insertions into the old fabric.

There are many aspects of barn lore, only some of which we now remember. Redwood (*Sequoia* species) or elm tree wood, for instance, becomes harder when it is wet. Hence, these woods are popular in Canada for constructing harbour quays and in Britain for lock gates. Each building material has its own special properties and today, as we use so much more softwood than hard, and more concrete and asbestos than brick or stone, we are forgetting a whole area of that instinctive knowledge which has equipped the humble barn to stand up for ever.

Certain words can explain particular basic conceptions – for instance, a small triangular 'wind-hole' in Anglo-Saxon times before the age of glass is the origin of 'window', now associated more with light than wind. The word 'barn' in Anglo-Saxon meant 'barley hall'. The Roman *aula* was an early 'hall' before houses were built as we know them today. The 'threshold' was a barrier of planks across the lower part of the porch, used to 'hold' back the grain when the chaff was turned in the air and blown out of the door by the wind.

Economy was usually a dominant factor for early builders just as it is today. Commonsense, therefore, often helps the more technical eye of the trained historian in dating a barn. Stones were frequently built only high enough to keep down the damp, with the main walls above this lower 'damp course' made of wood which was cheap and easy to work. The wood was replaced as it rotted, or as the barn was extended, so the higher parts of many walls are of a later date than the lower plinths. If a barn became larger and grander, the height of the stone might be increased for greater strength and, as at Egstow in Derbyshire, the lower tie beams might then be removed and used elsewhere leaving empty sockets in the stone wall.

Changes in fundamental structures are few and far between, but sometimes an arched wind brace will have a cusp or moulding that places it within a few decades. At Boxley, for example, the upper end of a stone interior course has a streamlined elegant cut-away taper, which occurs in recorded churches of about 1280: hence, this one small piece of precision carving, integral as it is to the whole colossal structure, offers a fairly precise

Stone plinths keep down the damp better than timber, but cost more. The main structure, therefore, is often timber, with stone beneath as here at Rogate, near Petersfield, Hampshire.

Straight edges on the timbers probably indicate softwood which became common after 1870, and machine sawing. Abbotsbury, Dorset.

date for the main building. Decorated roof trusses or moulded beams may tell a similar story.

There are various technical considerations which help to provide a general chronological scheme, at least by the century, if not by the decade. The most obvious is the introduction of softwood to the building industry in about 1870. Before that, barns used only the traditional hardwoods, mainly oak, chestnut, elm and ash. Spiders appear to dislike Spanish Oak which was used in the building of the fourteenth-century cloisters of Chichester Cathedral. Rats dislike Black Poplar and for this reason it was used in the building of some Essex barns where the prime grain for sale was stored, while ordinary grain for resowing was placed where it was accessible but vulnerable, in seed bins between the midstreys (porches). Softwood has none of these properties or romance. It was frequently used to replace old hardwood floors and beams in partially dilapidated barns and can often be recognized not only by its colour but by its shape — it was formed by machine, so its lines are straight and its angles sharp, unlike the earlier hand-worked hardwood.

Nails are another significant interior feature. They were little used before the nineteenth century: the big medieval barns, like Boxley, were built

An early medieval joint at Belchamp St Paul, Essex. Round pegs in square holes suggest rebuilding. Nails were not used before c.1800.

A primitive scarf-joint. The lower portion would be built first, thus indicating the order of building. Belchamp St Paul, Essex.

without a single nail. Pegs and wedges (known as keys) were the rule, with thorns for the roof and tiles, and very well they held too. They could not rust, and a judicious taper provided enough friction to keep them firm. A square peg in a round hole indicates some sort of rebuild or alteration.

A useful clue tells simply which end the barn building started. The horizontal beams, purlins, plates and puncheons, seldom extend the full length of the barn: where they join there is usually some form of overlap, and the later piece of timber would always be placed on top. Thus, the upper and lower portions of the scarf joints often indicate the order of building. A big medieval barn like Beaulieu, Hampshire, might have taken thirty years to build and lower standards can sometimes be found at the later end.

Wood frames were usually assembled laid flat on the ground, then hoisted into a vertical position. Only thus could mortice joints at the top be really tight, with no space for air round the socket. Where a mortice is too big for the tenon fitted into it, the implication is not only poor workmanship: assembly may have been effected in the vertical position, after the walls were completed, not before.

The barn at Frocester near Gloucester affords a superb example. In the original fourteenth-century roof there are no crevices round the sockets

Outside, unchanged and regular, c.1300. Frocester, Gloucestershire.

— they fit tightly for maximum strength; but in the portion which was rebuilt in the sixteenth century, the play that was necessary for construction high up *in situ* resulted in open, almost slovenly joints.

Ridge beams running the length of the roof inside its highest angle where the rafters meet became commoner only after the mid-eighteenth century and are a feature of some regions; perhaps the smaller timbers being used at that time gave less stability and therefore needed the extra strength provided by this additional member. At Lains Barn outside Wantage, the eighteenth-century roof has no roof-ridge beam, whereas in the nineteenth-century portion, the ridge plays a vital part, giving longitudinal stability now perhaps necessary because the other timbers are not so well assembled as in the earlier part.

A useful hint to the date of a barn can sometimes be spotted from the nature of the junction between purlin, post, tie beam and rafter, which varies, however, according to the region as well as to date. See glossary drawings.

Joints have become a new, specialized science of their own. John Harvey the medieval historian, first drew attention to the name of medieval carpenters in cathedral records. He and Cecil Hewett, the specialist in barn and church roofs, then attached some of these names to known existing works both in wood and in stone.

Inside the barn at Frocester, the roof shows signs of damage and reassembly because the sockets are unnecessarily big. When originally assembled on the ground no crevices between the beams would have been visible.

A typical 14C roof with magnificent timbers. The absence of a ridge beam suggests, in the south, an early date. Court Farm, Falmer, East Sussex.

OPPOSITE
One of the great medieval roofs, unusual with double tie beams and a ridge beam. Middle Littleton, Hereford and Worcester. National Trust.

The horizontal 18C purlins are cut into the rafters, a typical formation. Lains, near Wantage, Berkshire.

RIGHT
Northern building was usually smaller than in the south because the agriculture was poorer. Ridge beams were normal in the north in the Middle Ages. Aisles were often used for cattle. East Riddlesden Hall, near Keighley, West Yorkshire. National Trust.

OPPOSITE
The fatter end of medieval posts was put at the top where the greatest stress would occur. Alciston, East Sussex.

From this point in historical research, it was a short step for Cecil Hewett to develop a complete system of appreciating and dating the carpentry wizards of the roof. The key with which he unlocks these mysteries is the scarf-joint – the joint by which the long horizontal members are continued, almost imperceptibly, from one timber into the next. A big barn may be 150 feet long: a good beam may be 20 feet, so down either side there may be some fourteen beams to be fixed on end, one to another. For the period from the end of the twelfth to the end of the sixteenth centuries, Hewett has been able to establish a sequence of joint construction which may enable him to date a roof more precisely than ever before.

The first English settlement of Knights Templars was in Essex at Temple Cressing. There, the Barley Barn has an open-notched lap-joint suggesting a date of about 1200. This joint went out of use around 1230. The superb neighbouring Wheat Barn has a hidden notched lap-joint of about 1255, an even more sophisticated carpentry development.

The shorter timbers of the fourteenth century lessened the strain on the joints, so the notched joint gave way to the weaker feather-wedge. In the fifteenth century the edge-halved joint was preferred, with bird-mouthed, bridled abutments.

Cecil Hewett is certainly inventive and resourceful. His poetic terminology is magnificent; he has changed the accepted dating for some timber roofs by as much as three hundred years. But is he right? Science says he is. Radio-carbon dating and dendrochronology – determining the age of wood by counting the number of growth rings in the grain of the wood – both confirm his dates wherever they have been used. But he and the other analytical processes have not often impinged on one another. The lingering suspicion against the Hewett diagnosis is simply one of quantity. Many of the joints in the buildings he has examined, such as the pre-Norman Conquest portions of the barn at Belchamp St Paul, Essex, are different from and more rudimentary than those in his speculations. The small areas he has identified are a minute proportion of the mass of the contemporary woodwork that has not been analysed. His methods represent cool order in barn building. The vast majority of early barn roofs built represent exciting disorder. Some of the beams Hewett has examined, like most old building materials, have been used over and over again in different places for different purposes. How can one piece of wood date a whole building? One can often observe that an old beam has been used before, utilizing a set of holes and notches which are now visible on it, but which are redundant in its present position. Perhaps the barn has been reconstructed round this old beam, as Hewett's theories imply. But it is surely more likely that the old beam was brought to a new barn, rather than vice versa.

In all history of art studies, the whole is more important than the parts:

Only a few interior timbers remain as traces of the origin of this pre-Conquest barn, subject of much research by Cecil Hewett, Professor Born and others. The steep pitch of the roof implies that it was once thatched. Belchamp St Paul, Essex.

OPPOSITE ABOVE
A hipped gable end is a good protection from rain. This fine, typical West Sussex barn, formerly near Billingshurst, has been demolished and its materials sold.

OPPOSITE BELOW
Thatching in progress in 1983 with Norfolk reed on a wagon shed/barn at Campsea Ashe near Woodbridge, Suffolk.

one cannot identify a Botticelli by the shape of a finger nail or the curl of a hair: it is the total spiritual value that counts, the manner and vision of the master, not simply his pigments. Similarly, one cannot identify a whole piece of silver simply by the hallmark: the shape and style of the silversmithing are the real deciding factor. But until the study of vernacular buildings enables us to see the whole more clearly, in the way that we now see a Gothic cathedral or a Tudor manor house, Cecil Hewett's diagnosis of the minutiae of carpentry is as valuable as it is stimulating.

The outside covering of a roof has often been renewed many times, frequently with a different material as the demands of economy changed and the limits of convenient geography for local materials extended. A steep roof pitch implies an original intention to thatch, because thatch is absorbent and must therefore shed its load of rainwater quickly before the rain soaks in too far. The steeper the pitch of thatch the more efficiently the stalks composing it will turn the water from the building beneath. Another characteristic of a thatch, is that the rafters will be far apart from each other; rafters are partly for weight-bearing and thatch, being light, requires fewer supports. Finally, a hipped or turned-down end to a gable or roof, may also imply thatch: wind and rain from underneath ruin thatch, and a hip protects the side of the top thatch junction from being outflanked by the weather.

Most thatch was simply straw, and it was often grown in a nearby field. This still happens today in areas where thatch is common, like Essex. Thus the provision of a new roof may take two years or more: the field must be provided, the corn sown and harvested before the roofing can begin, and thatching needs summer weather. Reed thatch is best because reeds are longer and less absorbent than straw. But most reeds come from Norfolk, so the cost of transport would have prohibited their use in early times. It is true that small amounts of reeds grow throughout the country but not sufficiently widely – those grown in Hampshire, for instance, are

A long medieval roof at Tisbury,
Wiltshire, recently rethatched.
The undulating ridge line indicates
great age.

The thatch on this huge roof at
Charleston Manor was
successfully replaced with tiles
c.1933 by Sir Oswald Birley,
painter. Litlington, East Sussex.

not enough to satisfy the thatching needs of that county. A thatched barn roof today may cost over twice as much as a tiled roof — one reason why so many thatched roofs are being replaced with tiles, and why the price of old tiles with their pleasing patina rises steeply every year. Skilled thatchers are scarce; they can sometimes be recognized by the traces they carry of falls from their slippery roofs: a broken pelvis or leg, or crooked walk.

Tiled roofs are often built at an angle of about 45 degrees. Tiles are more absorbent than slate; water can also seep in underneath them more easily. Tiles used to be hung in position with thorns, as at thirteenth-century Boxley, or with wooden pegs. Now metal nails are often used; these can rust, have no give to allow the tile to nestle down cosily onto its wooden batten, and can easily crack whatever they grate against.

Where suitable soft stone was available, big stone slates were the standard and traditional roofing material from the Middle Ages. Clay tiles became common, like bricks, from the eighteenth century. The new material for thatch — corn — would have been difficult to obtain where sheep were common; so in pasture areas, stone slates and clay tiles were used more than the cheaper thatch. Stone was readily available in the Cotswolds and Pennines so stone roofs are normal there.

Slate, like thatch, occurs only in some regions, principally Wales and Cumbria. It was not used outside those areas until the nineteenth century when improved transport made the movement of building materials practical. From then on, slate became increasingly popular, especially in areas close to the new canals, railways and roads; today, slates are sometimes replaced by a lack-lustre plastic substitute. The accepted pitch is about

The stone slated medieval roof at Great Coxwell was well restored with 'valley stones' curving under the angles, a local Cotswold skill. Lead gutters in the angles are mostly new. National Trust. Near Faringdon, Oxfordshire.

Roman walls support Britain's most exotic coloured medieval roof at Farningham, Kent.

Tiles, like bricks, became commoner after the 18C. Lains, Wantage, is a typical Berkshire 18C/19C barn, with big porches and hipped gables.

30 degrees; the flatter slate roof will make a saving in timber underpinning compared with the bigger timber areas needed for thatch or tiles. It was commonsense that made possible the miracle of permanence achieved by barn roofs.

It is often imagined that the main structure of most early buildings was of oak. This is probably true of the Middle Ages, for the simple reason that other species of wood were either not available or would not have survived. But since the beginning of the seventeenth century, elm seems to have become the most common hardwood in the southern Home Counties.

Littlehampton Granary at the Weald and Downland Open Air Museum in Singleton near Chichester, West Sussex, has a stone dated 1751 and its old neighbouring farm buildings still *in situ* have a more formal datestone for 1752. On dismantling the granary for rebuilding in the museum, no less than 80 per cent of the wood was found to be elm, the rest being oak, with cleft chestnut battens to support the thatch.

There are, therefore, two reasonable suppositions to make when dating a timber barn. The bigger the timbers, the older the barn; and a preponderance of oak, as at Titchfield, in Hampshire, means it is medieval, whereas the use of elm or chestnut, as in the later part of the roof at Boxley, may mean it is sixteenth-century or later. But there are no reliable rules – timbers were so often rebuilt or moved.

Dates on buildings often record not the original construction, but some improvement or alteration. Occasionally, barns will have a datestone above the entrance or in the gable. For instance, the barn at Church Enstone in Oxfordshire has a stone giving the very early date 1382.

In half a dozen examples, the datestone on the barns seems obviously appropriate: at Paston in Norfolk, the source of that valuable record of domestic life, the Paston letters, Sir John Paston must have been proud of his barn: the date 1581 appears prominently carved into it not once, but twice, over an entrance and in a gable end. The barn at Moor Court, Romsey in Hampshire, bears the date 1701. At Kilnsey Old Hall towards the top of meandering Wharfedale in North Yorkshire, a deep-cut stone on its barn says 1648, and there is a storage barn nearby whose style fits

Flat gradients suggest that the slating is original – it was common in the north-west. Yew Tree Farm with spinning gallery, near Kendal, Cumbria. National Trust.

Datestone 1581, Paston, Norfolk.

Perhaps the only barn with two datestones, indicating the great pride of the builder 'Sir W Pasto Knighte'. Paston, Norfolk.

Barn, probably 16C, within the medieval Old Hall at Kilnsey, North Yorkshire, on slope so the fodder can easily be thrown down to the animals.

that date, (as well as two tiny square medieval barns in the surrounding fields, precursors of the thousands of later Yorkshire field barns). At Con, iston Old Hall in the Lake District conversely, stones are dated 1630 and 1700, surely later than the splendid central storage hall with its long approach ramp and huge conical Lake District chimneys. Passenham on the borders of Northamptonshire and Buckinghamshire has a pair of splendid barns built at right angles to each other, almost reminiscent of

Ramp at centre leads to 15C barn within the big dwelling house. Coniston Old Hall, Cumbria. National Trust.

the beautiful disposition at Temple Cressing. One is a medieval tithe barn, and the other bears the convincing date of 1646.

Datestones on later barns are more common. By this time the fascination of a barn is often no longer so much in the soaring timber interiors, but more in the patterns and texture of the bricks and stone outside. Llangarron, a typical red-sandstone Hereford barn, which to the lay eye might be of almost any date from 1550 to 1900, is fixed for us by its datestone

of 1757. A good example of the late use of Sussex flint is seen in the neatly shaped pair of barns at Milton Street dated 1832. An equivalent crispness of outline is seen in the Lake District at High Brundrigg with an 1879 datestone. The sophisticated Norfolk and Shropshire brick perfor-ation styles can be compared in the walls at Sea Polling near Waxham on Norfolk's east coast dated 1740, at Alkington, north of Shrewsbury, dated 1793, and at the two barns at Alvanley nearby, of 1582 and 1871: the colour of the brick is different but the ventilation perforations surpris-ingly similar. These patterns were due partly to functional need, partly to the module of bricks and bonding.

Datestones often indicate not the date of origin but of extension or alteration or restoration. Here 1793 fits the style of the building and is evidently original. Alkington, near Whitchurch, Shropshire.

Architects and barns have traditionally not marched together. The farm is too unpretentious, the architect too self-conscious, to make a happy team. The few exceptions are, however, distinguished. There is the domestic scale Tremedda Barn in Cornwall, designed by George Kennedy in 1926; the long, low mid-nineteenth-century blocks probably by Lewis Vulliamy at Westonbirt, Gloucestershire; the small Gothic group in rich Dorset woodland at Bridehead, designed by Pugin's most famous pupil Benjamin Ferry; the eighteenth-century Indian fantasy at Sezincote, in Gloucester-

OPPOSITE
A typical Victorian barn with 1871 datestone. Alvanley, near Runcorn, Cheshire.

shire, by S. P. Cockerell; model-farm layouts at Holkham Hall in Norfolk associated with the Wyatts, at Shugborough in Staffordshire by
Samuel Wyatt, at Wimpole in Cambridgeshire by Sir John Soane, and
at Goodwood, in West Sussex, and also its dower house, by the Wyatt
family.

*Granite gives clear definition to
Cornwall's old barn outlines.
Tregarthen, near Zennor,
Cornwall.*

*Fine architect-designed group by
George Kennedy 1926. Tremedda,
Cornwall.*

*Architect-designed barns are rare,
and seldom fit the landscape as
cosily as this, probably by Lewis
Vulliamy c.1860. Westonbirt,
Gloucestershire.*

Perhaps most majestic of all is Sir Edwin Lutyens' statement in brick and chalk at Marsh Court near Stockbridge in Hampshire. Lutyens worked on this estate for about thirty years from 1901, continually adding to his initial schemes because his client and friend Herbert Johnson found commissioning Lutyens so rewarding. The mansion, according to Lutyens' biographer, does not grow out of the ground, although, like so many of Lutyens' buildings, it uses the local materials, chalk and brick. It is a magnificent *tour de force*, not a natural growth.

Two other long-lasting Lutyens' projects incorporate old barns perhaps more naturally than the sculptural, statuesque Stockbridge farm. The gardening partner of his early years was Gertrude Jekyll, and he worked with her on her home, Munstead Wood, near Goldalming, partly out of affection and love. Their warm relationship is reflected in the garden and its harmonious association with its barns, the main works there being finished in 1907. Perhaps of better architectural quality is the group of buildings at Great Dixter, East Sussex, built from 1910. Rather grander in scale, more romantic in situation than Munstead, the old and new at Great Dixter are almost indistinguishable, giving to its garden a rare permanence.

NATIONAL
OPPORTUNITY

THE PROBLEM

Rehabilitation used to be a dirty word among young architects. The opportunity for the new creations which they all wanted, depended on the creation of new sites, not the reuse of old. A banquet of pure novelty, so the argument ran, was certain to be better than a nibble at an old meal.

Vernacular buildings suffered with the rest. Some thirty years ago, the huge medieval tithe barn at Wilmington Priory, in East Sussex, rotted, burned and vanished with hardly a tremor. At Bishopstone nearby, the local farmer pulled down the village's principal eighteenth-century barn and left only the lowered, misshapen end walls to remind us of his villainous act. The big medieval barn at Coggeshall in Essex steadily declined from an impressive monument to a virtual ruin and only recently has restoration work been started.

One voice was consistently raised to uphold the dignity of barns and farm buildings – the Society for the Protection of Ancient Buildings (SPAB). In the 1930s the National Trust was proposing to destroy one of its great barns at Avebury. Lord Esher, the SPAB's jovial, battling Chairman, told the Trust's meeting the proposal was so disgraceful they would have to do their work in the middle of the night wearing masks, or they would destroy not only the barn, but the National Trust too. The barn survived.

Public opinion and economic recession have now together achieved a dramatic improvement. The financial profit from property development is no longer guaranteed and barely justifies the risk involved. Destruction of old buildings is less easy and less profitable than it was a generation ago. The public is showing that it cares more for its environment than do some professionals. Amenity and preservation societies are active everywhere and the National Trust, much the biggest organization of all, has a huge and record-breaking membership of over 1.1 million. London's Architectural Association in 1975 started a practical course to teach architects about conservation and restoration techniques. Comparable courses are now available at the Universities of Edinburgh, York, Liverpool, Leicester, Oxford, Bruges, Rome and Venice. The machinery for listing and protecting old buildings has begun at last to take note of neighbourhoods and farm groups, as well as of individual masterpieces by known designers. The rate of listing has been increased because the listing process has been delegated by the government to some private architects. The SPAB itself is making a new 'Domesday' list of barns.

The SPAB one-day Barns Conference on 24 September 1980 at Lains Barn, Wantage, was an encouraging milestone, attended by two hundred people who came from varied backgrounds. One of the speakers, the

Duchess of Devonshire, owns some two hundred barns in Derbyshire, and clearly demonstrated the absurdity of the pedantic application of modern building, and fire and health regulations to ancient stone structures. She wanted to use her barns as overnight shelters for fell walkers, yet only by calling them 'stone tents' could she make a tiny loophole in planning regulations for her visionary schemes. But the general opinion was clear: most delegates favoured the idea of converting barns, rather than letting them collapse or – the usual alternative – building cheap new bungalows instead.

The case, in 1981, of Lord Neidpath and the Cutsdean Lodge barns on the Stanway estate in Gloucestershire came as a nasty setback. This compact group of late eighteenth-century Cotswold-stone buildings includes a barn, cart-shed, stable and cottage, strikingly situated on rising ground one mile from the village of Cutsdean, uninhabited since 1921 and agriculturally redundant since 1950. The owners of the Stanway estate sought permission to change the farm buildings to residential use. The Cotswold District Council refused, principally on the grounds that only barns within villages should be converted, and that conversion in this case would involve intrusive new dwellings in open countryside.

The estate's case was powerfully supported by David Verey (expert on Cotswold architecture), by Jeremy Benson for SPAB, by the Council for the Protection of Rural England (CPRE), by the parish council, by the Country Landowners' Association, and by Gloucester Community Council. The District Council argued, however, that a converted barn was bound to be visually offensive, that the sites should be cleared and ploughed, or that the Lodge should be repaired at a cost of £50,000 as 'a habitat for barn-owls', or allowed to collapse, as ruins were 'an asset to the landscape'.

The inspector on appeal decided in favour of the District Council, identifying three issues on which to base his decision: first, 'whether any evidence of overriding agricultural . . . need has been provided to justify the conversion'; second, whether conversion 'would . . . affect the simple style and character' of the group; and third, 'access'. As the appellants had in no way based their case on 'agricultural need', the inspector naturally decided against them on this issue. On the second point, he thought that conversion would 'radically change the whole appearance of the simple farm buildings which blend so well within their open natural setting' because windows would have to be introduced. And he found the access objections sufficient. Permission to convert was refused.

The decision was deplorable: it was based on agricultural need, which was not the issue; it neglected the fact that collapse would change the whole appearance of the simple farm buildings much more radically than mere conversion; it ignored the possibility, arising from the grouping of the buildings around a central courtyard, that all windows could be inward-facing, leaving the character of the group, as seen in the landscape, unaltered.

John Smith, founder of the Landmark Trust which restores old buildings, and makes them habitable, recalled a relevant imbroglio in 1977, showing how ill-adjusted modern bye-laws are to old buildings:

> ... a barn with a round-house attached, which – rather untypical of us but it was in the right place – we turned into a hostel for people on courses, field studies and so forth. We happened to have the bye-law man and the fireman there simultaneously. This round-house had one opening, through which the horse used to come to work the gin. The fireman asked, 'What's that?' Our architect replied, 'A window.' The fireman said, 'A window is not a means of escape.' As it was at ground-floor level, the architect said, 'Right, I'll make it a French window with louvres'; whereupon the bye-law man said, 'A french window is a door and a door is not a means of ventilation.' Our architect was somewhat downcast, until the fireman said, 'If on the other hand you wall up the only other means of escape it will then divide the building into two halves and both sides will be too small to come within my regulations.'

British planning legislation is the envy of the world. Its ideas and its scope are laudable, its staffing and its vigilance are wholly admirable. But it is the detailed decisions at the bottom of the great pyramid which so often lead to despair.

THE ROUTE TO PRESERVATION: ARCHITECTS AND PLANNERS

The main practical hope for the survival of barns is to let people live in them, as they increasingly want to. There are several companies, organizations and architects who specialize in converting barns. SAVE, a voluntary campaign to preserve Britain's heritage, locates and publishes lists of useful old buildings which are unnecessarily neglected; their booklet *Tomorrow's Ruins* lists some, and it makes depressing reading, especially as some of these ruins might have had up to 50 per cent repair grant from the then Historic Buildings Council. The Royal Institute of British Architects (RIBA) has lists of interested architects. Many architects are now gaining experience in barn conversion and regional lists are obtainable from district planning authorities or national park authorities. Country Farm Holidays of Powick, near Worcester, rents out farm accommodation in barns to holidaymakers.

Richard Male converted his eighteenth-century barn, measuring 90 feet by 20 feet, on the edge of Loughborough in Leicestershire. At the end of the hard work, he said, 'I've got a house I like, but not much in the bank.' In 1979 he started a summer course at Loughborough University called 'Home Conversion, Extension and Renovation'. Ian Haggie also converted his own barn at Barton Lane, Old Headington, and as a trustee of Oxford Preservation Trust, tries to encourage the use of traditional country materials in this region where there are probably more conversions than anywhere else.

Too often, local planners are roused not by worry, when action could be useful, but by disaster, when it is too late. At Llanellen near Abergavenny, for example, it was only after the great barn burned down a few years ago that Cardiff Museum, at great expense, interested themselves in its ruins and found Roman columns and the products of Roman metalsmiths.

THE KEY TO SURVIVAL: THE LISTING OF HISTORIC BARNS

The general principles guiding permission to convert are clear. Barns within the 'envelope' of a big village will usually be allowed to become dwellings. Barns isolated in the country, which must be the majority, will usually be refused permission for conversion to a new use, unless they are listed as being of some special artistic or historic importance. To get a barn 'listed' is therefore often a vital step towards ensuring its survival. The general attitude of the 'listers' at the Department of the Environment is that remote barns are not included on the statutory list. Lists are the key to the possibility of conversion and survival of old barns, and everyone agrees that the existing lists are inadequate.

Northumberland may represent the trend of future planning: it is keen to stem rural depopulation and encourage rural industries, so sensibly favours conversion of barns for residential and light-industrial purposes.

If the building is of exceptional national importance, it may qualify for Grade I listing which it will share with buildings such as Westminster Abbey and Blenheim Palace. A Grade I building can never be altered or destroyed except as a result of an act of God or by the specific consent of the Secretary of State for the Environment. Grade II star implies some feature of special national, as opposed to local, interest; it can be demolished or changed only by consent of the Secretary of State for the Environment, who may delegate the decision to the local authority. Applications affecting ordinary Grade II barns are decided by the local planning authority and only exceptionally referred to the Secretary of State. The fact that a barn is listed at all, is more important than the exact grading. These grades are an indication of quality, rather than a precise legal definition.

New development in Green belt

It is a criminal offence to demolish or materially alter a listed building without consent and the penalty may be imprisonment or a fine, or both. The fine may be related to any financial advantage gained in consequence of the work. Similarly, it is an offence to carry out an act likely to result in damage.

Before a listed building can be demolished or altered externally (or internally of Grade II star), Listed Building Consent must be obtained from the local planning authority. A specific application for Listed Building Consent must be made even where the work would normally be a 'permitted development' for an unlisted building. All applications for Listed Building Consent are advertised on the site and in the local press, and in the case of demolitions, the national amenity societies are notified. The planning authority takes into consideration any representations received as a result of this publicity before determining the application. In cases of demolition, if the authority is minded to grant consent the Secretary of State must normally be notified, and he has twenty-eight days in which to decide. If Listed Building Consent or Planning Permission is refused by the planning authority, or granted subject to conditions, the applicant has the right to appeal to the Secretary of State.

A further possible provision for protection, is for a building to be scheduled as an Ancient Monument. Usually applied to uninhabitable archeological remains like Stonehenge, the machinery for scheduling does nevertheless occasionally apply to barns. A monument, to be scheduled, must be uninhabited, but there is no limitation to its date. The scheme, unlike that for listing, is highly centralized through the Secretary of State for the Environment, and, in the case of overlap, scheduling invariably takes precedence over listing.

Subsidies and finance: Re-erection

More important than lists and grades, however, is the level of subsidy. A farmer can normally be given at least 30 per cent of the cost of a new agricultural building, and that means a barn, by the Ministry of Agriculture and the European Economic Community (EEC). But these government agencies will normally contribute nothing towards the repair of an old barn. This is because the EEC will support what it considers new productivity, which implies new buildings. But the agricultural productivity of old buildings is deemed to be static, so they earn no repair subsidy. There are, therefore, throughout the country, farmyards with old barns decaying and in the same yards cheap new barns built partly with public grants.

One of the only slender hopes for subsidies for repair is from the impoverished local authority. In a few cases, like Hampshire and Essex, they are concerned about barns, but they usually have inadequate funds for the purpose. Another source could be the Historic Buildings and Monuments Commission but here barns compete with buildings designed by famous artists like Robert Adam and Christopher Wren. Thus there is, as the late S. E. Rigold, the enthusiast for vernacular, gloomily used to say, 'a big subsidy for destruction, an incentive against repair'.

There is a further factor discouraging proper maintenance, and that is the scrap value of the best of these great piles. Lains Barn by Wantage has about 28,000 tiles on its cow byre, which measures some 200 feet in length, comparable to the longest medieval barn roofs. Some 60 per cent of the tiles were reused, meaning that 12,000 were replaced. There were 18,000 feet of battening, and a quarter of a ton of tile pins. Whether kept or sold, this constitutes big business. The numbers and bulk are staggering. So is the price. At Lee Farm, near Billingshurst in West Sussex, five large seventeenth-century barns were sold for scrap; each one fetched around £36,000—£12,000 for the tiles, £12,000 for the timbers and £12,000 for the plinth walls in West Sussex brown stone.

There is also the possibility of removal. As early as 1932 a barn alighted in the centre of St Albans, no doubt to the surprise of the local residents. Water End Barn was moved to a position beside the City Hall. Also in 1932 Colonel Montgomery moved a sixteenth-century barn from Great Bardfield in Essex to Rotten End, near Shelford. Vita Sackville-West and Harold Nicolson did the same thing, dismantling their half-timbered barn in their first home at Long Barn, Sevenoaks, and rebuilding it at the top of the hill beside the house of which it became a part. Another good Kentish barn was moved to Balcombe in West Sussex in 1980. The result of these removals is rather suburban and bogus in character, both inside and out, because so much infill and fenestration is new, as are the staircases, galleries and doorways.

The most comprehensive removal may, however, have inspired the great Knebworth House traction-engine drama, master-minded by architects Donald Insall and Gerald Dalby. Inches at a time, over a period of weeks, in 1973, a team of puffing steam-traction engines pulled a whole Tudor barn of about 1600 on specially-made wheels over a mile of undulating ground. The destination was beside another tiled, weather-boarded twin. Now, Manor and Lodge Barns, together with some new wings and gables, make a harmonious group of cafeteria and restaurant to satisfy visitors to the ancient home of the Lyttons and the Cobbolds in Hertfordshire. The effect is better inside than out; old beams reflect their antiquity better than partly-renewed tiles and planks.

The North American appetite for picturesque appeal has helped a few

English barns to find new transatlantic homes. Two barns dated 1655 from Kent have been reborn at Don Mills, a suburb of Toronto in Canada, as a sumptuous four-bedroomed house. Another larger barn measuring 25 feet by 75 feet is at Salt Lake City in Utah in the United States. David Howerd, a New Hampshire architect, expects soon to import annu-ally as many as twenty old English barn frames, the timbers packed and numbered in 40-feet containers. He says,

> People see these English oak frames – built five hundred years ago – being reassembled as the cores of houses which will last another five hundred years. Then they look at their own homes which are falling apart after twenty years and ask themselves, 'How come?' Well, their homes are vinyl over cardboard over plywood. That's how come. In Europe it's the country artisans who were best: it's the farmhouse that lasts. The frames we get from England are hundreds of years old, but basically the timbers are as good as when they were first put up. A barn, you see, breathes very nicely. The chances of rot are very small. Once you've cleaned the oak with a wire brush, you wind up with a gorgeous patina. And, of course, the structures were built properly in the first place, with hand-cut mortices and oak pegs in the joints.

The motive for removing or exporting barns is clear: it is better to save an old building, even in modified form, than to condemn it to the ultimate degradation of falling down. The morality may be disputed – exporting a nation's heritage cannot be wholly admirable – but exporting is preferable to the alternative, which is decay leading to death.

HOW TO CONVERT A BARN INTO A DWELLING

What advice, then, should a future barn-dweller adopt? If the barn is in the country, choose one of great beauty, so the local planners will see its value and want it to survive even if it is not yet formally listed. They may even expedite its listing. If it is near a road, then the common official objections to conversion – the need for unsightly new access, the difficulty of making hygienic drains – will be less. Talk to the local planning officers before, not after, making formal applications to convert. Planners are mostly highly sympathetic to old buildings; if the intentions of the converter are known in advance to be aesthetically good, ensuring that the essence of the building will be preserved despite its change of use, then half the battle is already won.

In a town or village, planning consent for change of use is easier to obtain than in open country. It will depend upon the quality of the architecture concerned, not as in country areas, upon the planners' wish to preserve the countryside free of human habitation. Most planners will now agree that any conversion of an old barn in a village or town is better than none, because the barn occupies a key architectural position.

The degree of conversion chosen depends on the degree of comfort required. But barn-dwellers generally love the size and simplicity of their buildings. They should start by changing it as little as possible. There are now many conversions, both good and bad; some of the best are listed in the gazetteer of the appropriate area. One excellent model is the medieval barn at Hales near Beccles in Norfolk; already by the Middle Ages the major part was used as storage, with a dwelling and a partial intermediate floor at one end. Here is a medieval conversion which inserted small rooms in one end and left most of the big hall free for storage and agricultural use. Old ideas often weather best. Hales is one of the oldest and best examples of all.

The best conversions are those which retain the barn's essential character: its size, its space, its old materials, even its uneven mass. The least satisfactory conversions are those which subdivide the interior into many small rooms, and perforate the exterior with small domestic windows, thus giving a small-house feeling to a big-scale conception. As the Essex County Council barns report says, 'These often immense structures are the most impressive and important agricultural buildings this country has ever produced.' That is not the sort of description you apply to a bungalow, but many converters try to conceal the barn's main asset, its size, in order to conserve heat and cut the running costs of a large house.

Planning permission to convert into a dwelling may increase the value of a barn by double or more. The financial stakes, therefore, are quite high; the planning decisions may not only make or mar a barn, they may dramatically affect an individual's financial position as well.

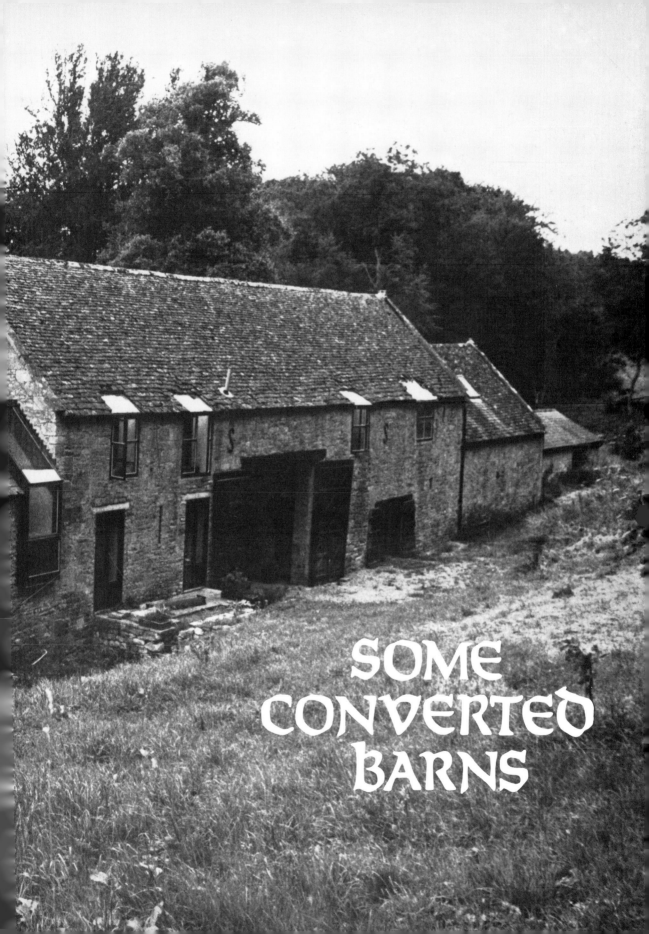

SOME CONVERTED BARNS

PREVIOUS PAGE
The sensitivity of the artist-owners is everywhere evident at Temple Guiting, near Stow-on-the-Wold, Gloucestershire.

There must be hundreds of conversions in progress now. To select a mere handful for discussion, as I have done, is obviously unfair, but each one is beautiful, each does what all conversions should do: it retains the essential mass and grandeur of the original barn. And each is almost unknown.

Great Bealings solar barn near Woodbridge in Suffolk, was converted in 1977–78 by Robin Sadler to his own design. He opens his barn to the public once a year and attracts at least five hundred visitors during that one day. This suggests he is not alone in caring for our environment, for preserving Britain's old buildings and for harbouring its energy. The barn, on the edge of its village, had been derelict for twenty years, which may partly account for the local authority's positively welcoming Robin's planning application. The date 1863 is boldly painted on one of the collar beams, but the barn is probably older – its style suggests the eighteenth century. It is of average size, about 70 feet long, weatherboarded, with a pair of big rust-coloured timber doors surprisingly and sensibly still in use, and a roof in local red pantiles. Rather unusually, it stands along the top of a bank by the road, not an easy entry for a loaded threshing wagon.

There the normality ends. Robin thought his conversion would cost about £16,000 and his guess was remarkably accurate for he actually spent £22,000. Most barn converters emerge from their ordeal visually thrilled, but financially much more bruised than this.

He wanted to use the sun to prove that we can almost live without those hydro-carbon fuels which are running short, and which cost so much; and he was determined to keep warm. He knows that most barn owners burn up vast quantities of oil for heating and still have to sit shivering in one corner of their huge rooms. His solar heating had to be effective.

He aimed to keep the outside looking big and bold as a barn should do, and at the same time have lots of light. His method was to leave the big threshing-door openings intact and to insert only a few other windows and skylights, all big and bold. The Sadlers also wanted a large room inside, so they left the centre as it was – uncluttered and enormous. Many city dwellers seem frightened of this inspiring emptiness when they get to their country barns, so they fit mezzanine floors throughout for cosiness, thus bringing town congestion to country space.

Robin is a visionary, not an architect, hence perhaps his triumph over conventional prejudice. Solar heat can, and does, work in rainy England, and in a vast uninterrupted internal space. His secret was simple and two-fold: insulation on the one hand, and a knowledge that sun will provide heat even through mist or cloud on the other: indeed, direct rays of sunlight are less efficient for heating than diffused rays. Robin obtains over half his winter heat from the sun; the other half comes from his wood-burning

The appearance, both in and out, is pure delight. One great asset of the solar system is that no big chimneys are needed – so many barn houses are ruined by new chimneys. The solar roof panels are on the field side of the barn and therefore invisible from the road. The greenhouse skylight is similarly shielded from the road by big old trees. The backside looks onto a small lawn with shrubs and vegetable garden, and within 20 feet of the back door, endless cornfields stretching to the horizon. The ground floor inside includes a garage at one end and a greenhouse the other, and, within the barn proper, kitchen and lavatory both at the same end under

Solar barn (for which the sun provides heating) at Great Bealings, Suffolk. Front view (above), seen from the fields at the rear (right) and inside view (opposite).

one pair of bedrooms. The main central area stretches under the other bedrooms, giving a low-ceilinged intimate sitting space, with a bold open staircase where it debouches into the barn's full height. Some of the principal rafters and the collars are left revealed. They give with their dark colour, a fine contrast to the modern oak, sycamore, beech and pine. Throughout, the variety of these natural colours is very pleasing. The old bricks and tiles complete a simple but subtle study in space and texture.

Another splendid medium-sized barn conversion is at Fifield near Burford in Oxfordshire. The barn is built of glorious honey-coloured

Cotswold stone. The owners are Leslie and Rosamund Julius, lately heads of the world-wide Hille furniture business founded by Rosamund's grand-father. Two generations of British modern designers owe them a big debt for their constant encouragement of new ideas. Feeling for style and quality may be seen in their trade showrooms in London, and their barn, which they finished in 1980, reflects the same sense of perfection.

The interior is entirely open upstairs, and downstairs there is no more than a semi-enclosure for kitchen and services. A gallery at first floor level each end provides an enclosed bedroom and an open-terrace sleeping space one end, a big play area the other, with a wall gangway joining the two and spiral staircases giving access. A bench round the ground-floor walls, conceals the central heating pipes and provides casual seating, while the big square wood-burning stove and its meandering shiny flue are the focus both of warmth and fun. There is nothing more beautiful in the evenings than the sight of naked flames leaping in an open fire, and Leslie has fixed the fire almost at eye level — the right level to see the flames easily. All around are powerful heavy modern tables and chairs, lamps and shelves, pictures and sculpture (a memorable piece by the Mexican Hugo Rodriguez) — straight, honest design is what barns need, and that is what the Juliuses have provided. Entering the barn from the tiny rooms of the cottage is a liberating surprise.

Outside, the feeling is unpretentious and solid. The threshing doors have been partly walled up leaving vertical window apertures, an exterior sacrifice for an interior gain, as the views of the village around are more practical than elevating. The small surrounding gardens each provide their own suntrap, their own different aspect and prospect, but the success at Fifield is not a generous outside spectacle: it is a secret internal drama.

A third extraordinary barn conversion is at Hatfield Broad Oak near Dunmow in Essex. It is, like, the solar barn at Great Bealings, a timber barn but it is much longer at 135 feet, listed in Grade II, and aisled with big fifteenth-century timbers inside. In 1971 a successful architectural group — Architects' Co-partnership — having decided to leave London, bought it, with outline planning permission, to convert into three dwellings: three of the partners, two architects and an engineer, formed a trust and converted it for their own use. The building works included the removal of some modern outshots and alterations, stripping and recovering the weatherboarded walls and the plain tiled roof, and underpinning the foundations with a reinforced concrete raft — many old barns have no foundations at all, being laid on top of the soil, not into it, rather like a big marquee. Perhaps this is the reason their timbers seem impervious to damp — the timber and the damp simply never meet. The main building took only nine months, the outbuildings another four months, and the job was finished in 1974, by P. Francis & Co., builders of Thaxted.

Open modern interior in the traditional Cotswold barn at Fifield, near Burford, Oxfordshire (above), and pleasing exterior (left).

Major rebuild still preserves the original outline. Hatfield Broad Oak, Essex.

The sloping gardens are still establishing themselves but will form a leafy sanctuary. Work is now starting on similar treatment to the adjoining barns.

Inside, the barn was divided by party walls at the third and the sixth bays, the weight of the new half upper floors, containing bedrooms, being taken by these walls on the new raft foundation. The living rooms, on the garden side, reveal the full height of the barn up to the collars, including the principal posts with enormous jowls, and diagonal three-way braces, tie beam, collar crown post, and curved arch braces. As usual in a medieval barn, there is no central ridge beam along the interior top of the roof and, rather unusually, there are no wind braces in the plane of the roof, perhaps suggesting a date earlier than the fifteenth century. The wood stoves with their big flues, lead the eye up to a first-floor interior gangway running between the bedrooms. It is all pleasing, neat and orderly. The conversion keeps the barn's full height in a few places where you can see the fascinating medieval carpentry but it has perhaps, in losing the interior length to a series of smallish rooms of square section, lost its soul, which is simply its feeling of endlessness.

A fourth good conversion to record is in North Yorkshire at Keldwick, Thornthwaite near Harrogate, a 200-year old Yorkshire stone barn, converted by Mrs Chris Ramsay in 1975, winner of a Civic Trust house and cottage award in 1975 – rare distinction for a mere barn. The central room uses the entire height and width, which is about 20 feet square and 22 feet high in the centre. The kitchen-dining space is 28 feet by 16 feet, while the whole building is only about 70 feet long. Its exterior still looks like a barn with the threshing doors filled in with glass, the other windows erratically placed, not regimented. The tie beams, purlins, collars, queen posts and struts look very strong from floor level, and are better integrated to the space available than the old timbers are at Hatfield Broad Oak, for the simple reason that the ceiling area in the big room seems bigger in proportion to the timber scantlings.

SOME CONVERTED BARNS

*Almost no alteration to the
exterior of this traditional
Yorkshire barn was necessary to
make it a fine dwelling (left).
Interior view (below). Keldwick,
near Thornthwaite, North
Yorkshire.*

One of the most important sites in East Sussex at Wilmington. Place Barn – interior before and after conversion (below and opposite); exterior view (opposite above).

The new floor of African Muhuhu strips appears to be as indestructible as the old York stone walls. What is especially pleasing, again in contrast to the more sophisticated and smooth-walled Hatfield conversion, are the bare stone blocks which form the outer walls, and which have not been plastered over. A steel open-tread staircase (very suitable for a barn) leads up from the music room to a gangway connecting the six bedrooms and studies on the first floor. There is constant surprise as one room leads to another of quite a different scale, each with stimulating glimpses onto the fields around. Panorama windows would have cheapened the view by revealing it all at once, and spoiled the building by destroying the robust solidity of the stone walls.

The ideal barn conversion leaves a big interior room, preferably in the middle between the threshing doors, as at Great Bealings, Fifield or Keld-wick. But big rooms are difficult to heat, more for dreaming than for

living. Anyone in a big barn room will tend to talk more of the fine timbers, the feeling of release, the extension of country liberty into the confines of home, rather than of the intimacy of a warm fire on a winter's evening and curling up on a sofa to read a good book.

A good compromise, combining the feel of a big room with the comfort of a small foyer, has been achieved at Wilmington in East Sussex. Like most new projects for old buildings, it involved a planning battle, particularly because the view from the barn is among the best in Sussex — of those curving, bulbous hills, the South Downs, and, to punctuate the centre is the Long Man of Wilmington, a giant figure carved out of the turf in silhouette, on Windover Hill. Nearby is the fifteenth-century gatehouse of the Priory and beside the Priory ruins is a larger barn which has been converted.

The previous owner, Mrs Gwynne of the ancient Sussex landowning family, watched helplessly as some of her barns here first became useless and then decayed. The local authority refused permission to convert the remaining barns.

At this point, Mrs Gwynne evolved a compromise deal with the planners who would let her convert two derelict barns if she allowed a car park on the site of the third demolished tithe barn. Eventually she refused: the country, she believes, is for people and not for cars, and she regretfully sold her estate. The car park was built and the two barns were duly modernized.

Temple Guiting, near Stow-on-the-Wold, Gloucestershire. Stone threshing floor left intact (opposite).

Anne de Geus owned the smaller of them and adopted a modified big-room policy, dividing her big room by a new wall with a huge open fire. She built bedrooms upstairs one end, her husband's study the other, and she retained the full interior height with the roof rafters and beams in the two big central rooms. She invented her own own cladding of damp plaster to secure the powdering old cement in the flint walls. She used old timber above the central fireplace so the central wall could easily be taken also for old. The big threshing doors are now sheets of $\frac{1}{2}$-inch glass giving a fine prospect of the Priory ruins on one side and Windover Hill the other. The planners had still another brick to throw – they required three, instead of the original two, windows on the south side, because three would look less like a dwelling. Strange conception – that new windows would look older than the old.

The best epic conversion is an artist's dream at Temple Guiting near Stow-on-the-Wold in Gloucestershire. Jeremy and Lyn le Grice spent two years restoring their large barn with their own hands and it may be the most satisfying of all the barn conversions considered. The rooms are mostly smaller than at Hatfield Broad Oak, so there are plenty of creature comforts, yet the varieties of space used are as stimulating as at Keldwick, producing many exciting architectural experiences, and the interior, being home-made, has a splendid personality of its own!

An original feature of the building is the open passage formed between the threshing doors. On one side, the door opens onto a huge playroom the full height and length of the old barn, from which a rough Victorian staircase ascends to what was Jeremy's painting studio on the first floor at one end. Opening the other way from the massive stone threshing floor are the living rooms. They are punctuated by huge oak beams, perhaps of around 1600, and lumps of stonework, probably medieval. Part of the first floor in this portion is new, and lies at the top of the enchanting exterior stone staircase which was part of the original granary. There are beautiful views of the towering beech trees above and the monk's fishpond below. The whole scene is sylvan, with shrubs and flowers everwhere.

Lyn's studio, from which she conducted her successful worldwide art-stencil campaign, was in one of the old cowsheds.

For the intending barn-dweller, there are basic questions to decide: is a big sheet of plate glass the best way to cope with the threshing door

opening? It is the most beautiful solution, yes, but also the most public. Is a single big room inside as at Fifield, the only way to be honest with the building, or should one be honest with oneself in preference, and provide some small rooms from which hot air will not rise too quickly? The biggest rooms are visually best, but barn lovers who shiver with cold, are not the best advertisement for the attractions of conversion. How can windows be placed most advantageously to light the inside, most discreetly to preserve the outside? Skylights in the roof seem very desirable because they keep the all-important roof line. In the walls, some form of erratic distribution of windows may be demanded by the structural details, as at Temple Guiting, and usually variety suits country buildings better than regular symmetrical dispositions as at Hatfield Broad Oak. Symmetry tends to suggest the town. How much interior timber looks right? Old wood beams and rafters, and their often weird coordination, are the chief glory of a barn. How liberating when one can see all the soaring lines as in

Camping barns of the Countryside Commission at Camhouses. The Yorkshire moors and old barns need the use which hikers can bring. North Yorkshire.

the various agricultural museums like Michelham or Brook, or at least most of them as in the homes at Wilmington, Fifield or Great Bealings. The fullest exposure of the original fabric is what gives the greatest pleasure.

In the future, either conversion or ruin will be the choice. At London's Royal Society of Arts on 21 November 1984 a distinguished one-day barns conference, chaired by the Duke of Gloucester, heard with consternation of the poverty of our planning laws, and the plight of our barns. Perhaps the Countryside Commission will succeed in its brilliant visionary dream of creating as many as twenty thousand camping barns or bunkhouses, thus proving to farmers throughout the extensive national parks, that rent from their old barns can be more profitable than small-scale dwindling agriculture on the moors. Perhaps in time barns will come to house more campers than cattle, shedding happiness as well as beauty from their rugged forms. Conversions of all sorts are bound to become more common and better organized. They must and should be generally welcomed.

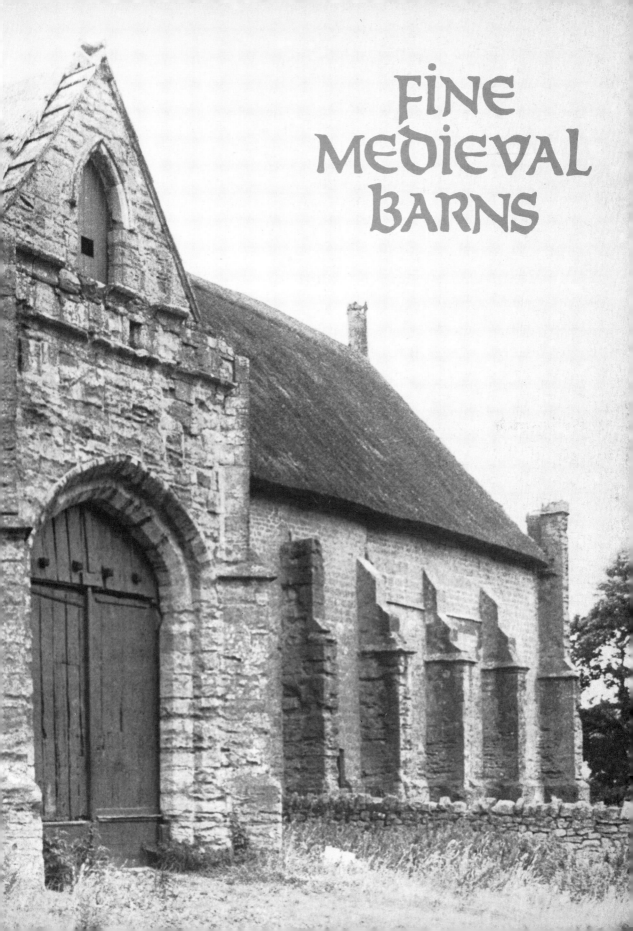

FINE MEDIEVAL BARNS

PREVIOUS PAGE
Abbotsbury, Dorset. The Great Barn of Abbotsbury Abbey was built c.1400. Once stone-slated, it is now thatched.

Stone medieval barns occur mostly in the south and west of England. They have a family likeness one to another, much as our cathedrals have comparable magnificence. They have never before been reproduced together, with their artistic and historical features summarized. This chapter and its illustrations, with those which have been placed on previous pages to illuminate relevant points in the text, should therefore fill a serious gap. Much research remains to be done, especially in cartularies and monastic records. At present, we know the history in some detail of only a few medieval barns. Other barns, often of equal or greater architectural splendour, have no recorded pedigree; their pictures here should at least serve as a reminder of these great, but still largely unknown British building triumphs. For the first time we can now dream of a comparative standard in matters of style and size.

Medieval barns built of flint or wood are more difficult to date than those built of shaped stone; only a few of the grandest are therefore given in this chapter, the remainder finding their due place in the gazetteer of the regions.

Big medieval barns are few and far between. In Devon at Torre Abbey, Torquay, is the fine Spanish Barn. Within its massive rough-hewn walls, almost four hundred Spanish soldiers and sailors from the Spanish Armada were imprisoned after their ships had been driven ashore at Torbay in 1588. The barn's inhabitants today are an altogether happier lot – it is used as an occasional summer theatre, surrounded by the municipal pitch-putt golf course.

Torquay, Devon. Torre Abbey, c.1300.

Buckland Abbey was the last monastery founded in Britain by the Cistercians, and the most westerly in the country. Endowed by Amicia, Countess of Devon, with a tract of the royal forest on the edge of Dartmoor, it was begun in 1278 and finished about 1300. The Abbey employed many laymen or *conversi*, building up a local labouring population. By 1290 the village which belonged to the monks, was known as Buckland Monachorum (Buckland of the monks). There were only twelve monks, yet this small group organized the building of a huge, splendid barn, no less than 150 feet long 32 feet wide and 60 feet high. Its ambitious scale and fine workmanship are reminders of the monks' economic and social power: the Abbot administered local justice and sustained his rights as administrator of an important estate. Buckland was also concerned with defence: in 1336 the Abbot petitioned the Crown for the right to embattle the Abbey and the barn against marauding Bretons who were pillaging along the Devon coast. The wall slits in the barn, primarily for ventilation, had a military purpose too.

The barn still has its original timber roof with a fine, generous internal arch, the huge vertical members resting directly on the timber plates along the top of the walls. The comparable construction at Bradford-on-Avon has had recent repairs because the weight of the roof pressed the walls outwards, necessitating underpinning and the insertion of iron cross ties.

Buckland Abbey, Devon. 'Tithe' barn built c.1300. Thatch replaced by slate in 1772. Approximately 150 × 32 feet, and 60 feet high; no nails or screws.

Not so at Buckland. Perhaps the hard granite made it stronger. More likely, it was the close intervals between the outside buttresses – an unusual feature shared with the Spanish Barn at Torre, Torquay, – that gave stability to the loosely constructed walls. The roof was built entirely with wooden pegs, without screws or nails; originally thatched, it was covered with local slate in 1772, an additional weight which might have over-whelmed less lavish scantling.

Middle Littleton, *c.*1220, provides a useful lesson in restoration. The great stone slate roof was restored twice in the 1970s and it still leaks. The slates were reseated too precisely, by craftsmen who were not familiar with the local traditions of building: local craftsmen would have hung the slates more loosely, making the necessary allowance for the inevitable give under the weight of stone. Bredon, near Tewksbury, is another of Britain's best medieval barns. Its outside staircase leading to the watch-man's room, or *grangarius*, is especially rare. In 1981, the roof was destroyed by fire but the main vertical oak posts were little damaged, being hardened with age and almost impervious to fire; the rest of the roof was well repaired, and is a tribute to modern craftsmanship.

In 1204 King John granted the Manor of Faringdon in Oxfordshire to the Cistercians of Beaulieu, who soon formed a cell at Great Coxwell and there erected before 1250 a huge barn, which, after the Dissolution passed to private ownership, and 1956 to the National Trust. It became one of William Morris's favourite buildings and he was not the only lover of this little-known masterpiece. Frank Lloyd Wright, the great American architect, came to England in the 1950s to receive the gold medal of the Royal Institute of British Architects. During his visit his British hosts asked which building he would most like to see. His choice surprised them: it was the barn at Great Coxwell.

William Morris's home at Kelmscott Manor in Kelmscot is surrounded by a nest of seventeenth- and eighteenth-century barns: three in his Home Farm, one medieval, one red-brick, one with a stone dovecot, and over a dozen in the small village of Kelmscot. But this was not enough for him, the first great barn enthusiast. He often walked his visitors over the fields to Great Coxwell to see what he said was 'the finest piece of architec-ture in England, as beautiful as a cathedral.'

The main posts are 22 feet 6 inches high: they rest on stone plinths nearly 7 feet high, their bases capped with oak templates as a sort of damp-course. The building has remained almost unchanged for over seven cen-turies. In 1868 four of the tie beams were reinforced by planks of deal bolted along them – a typical cheap, modern softwood repair. All the rafters, except in the north bay, were also renewed in deal. In 1961 and 1962 complete stripping and reconditioning of the heavy Cotswold-stone roof was undertaken by the National Trust.

Less happy but hardly less magnificent is Frocester in Gloucester, 186 feet long and 30 feet wide, compared to Great Coxwell's 152 feet by 44 feet. In the nineteenth century it belonged to the Hayward family; they were agricultural innovators and it was probably they who built the important neighbouring series of grouped Victorian barns. These are strong architecturally and typical of the region. Other examples are the large nineteenth-century barns at Beer, Gloucestershire, and Westonbirt nearby.

The long, low Great Barn at Frocester was built between 1284 and 1306 for the Abbot John de Gamages. The walls are made of local oolitic limestone; the roof of local stone slates, 26 inches long at the eaves diminishing in courses to $6\frac{1}{2}$ inches at the ridge. There are thirteen bays and, exceptionally, two wagon porches, both on the same side, and none on the other. Frocester was purpose-built but the owners evidently did not require the classic drive-through arrangement.

In Sussex the big timbers in Alciston's flint barn indicate a medieval date, probably fourteenth century. It is like near-by Falmer in that its exterior is free of modern sheds or outshots; some of its walling is recent, of the eighteenth or nineteenth century; its surroundings are superb, with trees to shade it and, to illuminate its great scale, endless fields sloping up to Firle Beacon.

In Essex, foremost among the landmarks is the marvellous group at Temple Cressing. This was the earliest English settlement of the Knights Templar, who were given the manor in 1135. When they were suppressed, the property descended in 1312 to the Hospitallers. Then in 1512 the farm became private property. The two barns there are splendid inside as well as out. Both are aisled, with half-hips at the end and gables in the upper portion. The third great building of the group is a grand sort of guest house, which is whitewashed and half-timbered, and dated 1623, indicating that prosperity continued after the knightly crusading orders had finished. It's a fine group with its farmhouse, garden wall and moat.

Another barn, in Essex, typical of its age, is at Widdington. It has large porches, a central roof ridge beam, a tiled roof, weather-boarded walls, and five windows cut in on the porch side possibly in the nineteenth century. Several similar barns are falling down today. Its interior timbers with ogee-shaped support braces for the crown post, and shaped jowls and knees to accommodate and support the right angle changes in direction, are rarer. All these features indicate the great period of English architecture, namely the Decorated style of the fourteenth century. This richness of style may have been extinguished, together with the prosperity which brought it into being, by the Black Death after 1348. The finest carpentry may have begun to vanish with the Black Death too: the scarf-joints, stop-splayed and sallied, each with pegs and keys, were economical of timber and very strong.

Widdington Barn has been sketched and painted by Sir George Clausen, the distinguished painter who lived in the village until 1905. He was one of the first artists to record agricultural work systematically: threshing and flailing, scything and sorting, all were given a prominent place by his palette. Barn interiors were one of his favourite subjects. The artist in him liked the strong chiaroscuro, the idealist saw in the heavy style of the buildings a fine expression of intellectual honesty and fitness for purpose, so dear to his friends in the Arts and Crafts movement.

Widdington's history is quite a saga. William the Conqueror gave land here to the nuns of St Valéry to thank them for their prayers. This spiritual help had secured for him a favourable wind to bring him across the English Channel with his invasion army. The Abbey Farm at Widdington was built on this land. Its surviving medieval stone wall, its monks' fishpond and moat, and its big barn, make it a memorable architectural group.

The barn became derelict and was given to the Department of the Environment in 1975 by its owner Jeremy Dillon-Robinson. The Department indulged in some expensive and expert first aid, revealing good threshing floors made of stone between the entrances, but a paucity of joints in the longitudinal plate beams to help with dating.

Then panic seems to have set in. Some rumour that barns are impossible to repair must have ruffled the calm in Whitehall. An expensive scaffold frame was spread throughout the interior, an equally mint-condition corrugated iron umbrella opened above the barn's medieval roof skeleton, and all work suddenly stopped, not to be completed until 1983 by a private firm of builders. The barn is now open to the public.

At Witham, Essex, on the road from Braintree to Chipping Hill through Hawbush Green, is Powers Hall Farm, perhaps dating from the early fifteenth century. The roof outside was once thatched. Inside, it is spacious and splendid. The elegant wind braces in the plane of the roof stop the rafters falling sideways or 'raking' as they have done in the earlier roof at Widdington.

Twenty miles away is the site of a great barn drama, in the centre of the superb village of Coggeshall, also in Essex. The Grange Farm there had a famous timber and brick barn, about 130 feet long, with king posts, six bays, aisles, two porches and a huge tiled roof. Coggeshall Abbey was founded by King Stephen in about 1140 and became Cistercian in 1148. The whole complex has astonishingly early brickwork, some of the earliest in the country; the bricks, according to medieval records, were made on site.

The Great Barn used to dominate the skyline for about 850 years. The owner-farmer claimed he spent £300 annually maintaining it, but decided it was useless and wanted it removed, although it is a Grade II listed

building. The Environment Secretary in 1978 refused permission to demolish it. The town Amenity Group felt the barn should stay.

By June 1978 the owner had installed notices saying 'Dangerous Structure', and there was a local lament at the 'toothless' law which made
the preservation of listed buildings discretionary rather than mandatory.

An American visitor to England wrote to the Secretary of State:

> As a foreign visitor who has been to Britain many times I cannot under-
> stand British logic. I note the great consternation of British people at
> foreigners' purchase of art objects not created by British artists and
> purchased by wealthy British in the past or captured in wars. They are
> called part of the British heritage, and considerable effort is made to retain
> them in Britain. They are mostly recent additions, by purchase or conquest.
> But the British people are largely unconcerned with the preservation of
> their true heritage, such as the 850-year-old Great Barn at Coggeshall.
> This is a work of British artisans that symbolizes the very best in the British
> heritage and has served the people throughout the centuries. Yet it will
> be permitted to rot or to be moved from its own habitat!

An English architect and vernacular enthusiast, John Weller, says he
watched the decay with 'impotent rage'. The three early bays still surviving
looked a sad relic of its former spaciousness. The compulsory purchase
order issued in 1983 resulted in its complete restoration.

Leiston Abbey Barn, not far from Aldeburgh on the Suffolk coast,
represents perhaps the epitome of East Anglian agricultural wealth, being

*Leiston Abbey Barn, Suffolk,
c.1400.*

the centre of employment in its region. Built soon after the abbey's foundation, after the fire in 1380, it is of brick, stone, chalk and flint. Its splendid high-pitched thatched Norfolk reed roof (recently renewed) has a bold patterned skyline. The barn stands alone in its field, high and strong, near the big abbey ruins. Inside, its simple tie beam and collar roof with no struts or vertical braces or posts, make it well suited for its new use as an uncluttered, aisleless assembly and concert hall, and it made a fine setting for a barn dance for the visitors to the Aldeburgh Festival in 1979. Its lack of big doors must have diminished its usefulness to the farmyard behind.

The finest Midlands medieval barn, 150 feet long and 34 feet wide, cruck-framed, and brick-clad, early fourteenth century, is at Leigh Court about 5 miles west of Worcester. There are eleven pairs of crucks about 35 feet long — the end ones are shorter, ending at the collars where the half-hipped roof begins its inward slope. The roof is built partly of old hand-made tiles and partly new replacement tiles, while some of it has

Leigh Court Farm barn, at Leigh near Worcester, Hereford and Worcester. The biggest surviving cruck-framed barn, now (1984) in danger; early 14C.

collapsed. This is a great barn, which is steadily decaying despite sympathetic words from the Department of the Environment.

The surrounding farm includes several very big square oasts with pyramidal tops, a type which seldom yields in this region to the smaller round cone tower as it did in Kent. Leigh Court altogether makes one of the country's great barn symphonies, comparable with Tisbury, Toller Fratrum, Buriton, Little Bedwyn, Alciston and Temple Cressing.

- There are, however, two big stone groups further north still, in Yorkshire. East Riddlesden Hall, the National Trust haven on the edge of Keighley, has two barns by their pond. The earlier of them probably has medieval timbers with their squat, craggy outline and directness of function.

At Bolton Abbey, the barn with its aisles and its roof descending quite close to the ground, is one of the biggest and most imposing in the country. It seems to have medieval timbers within, though the several carpentry systems show signs of later changes. The walls and roof must have been at least partly rebuilt in the eighteenth century, to judge from their style. But the stately proportion of the whole suggests the confidence of a wealthy monastery. Perhaps like Bolton Abbey itself across the field, the barn was begun as early as the twelfth century. Anyway, the strength of its architecture makes up for the uncertainty of its date, and it is a fitting end to this quick journey through the finer medieval barns of Britain.

East Riddlesden Hall, near Keighley, West Yorkshire. National Trust. The squat shape implies an aisled barn.

OPPOSITE ABOVE
*Tisbury, Wiltshire. One of the
longest medieval barns.*

OPPOSITE BELOW
*Ashleworth, near Gloucester,
Gloucestershire. 1481–1515.*

ABOVE
*Preston Plucknett, Somerset.
One of a fine group around
Glastonbury, all c.1400.*

LEFT
*The Great Barn of Abbotsbury
Abbey, Dorset, c.1400.*

RIGHT AND OPPOSITE
Bredon, near Tewkesbury,
Hereford and Worcester. National
Trust, c.1300.

RIGHT
Bretforton, near Evesham,
Gloucestershire, c.1220.

BELOW OPPOSITE AND
BELOW
*Siddington, Gloucestershire.
Typical Cotswold barn c.1300,
built when the Cotswolds
dominated Europe's wool industry.
Recent applications to demolish
withdrawn after protests.*

OPPOSITE ABOVE AND
BELOW
*Boxley, near Maidstone, Kent,
c.1300.*

BELOW
*Doulting, c.1400, one of the great
Somerset group of medieval barns.*

*Stoke-sub-Hamdon, Somerset,
c.1400, part of a big group.
National Trust.*

OPPOSITE ABOVE
*Westenhanger, Kent. Medieval
stonework with fine interior and
spectacular setting on racecourse.*

OPPOSITE BELOW
*Waxham, Norfolk. Huge
medieval barn with beautiful
patterning on walls.*

RIGHT
*Wells, Somerset. Bishop's Barn,
c.1400. One of a distinctive
Somerset group. Now used for
public meetings.*

Woodspring Priory, near Weston-super-Mare, Avon, c.1300. The Abbey was built to expiate the sin of the murder of St Thomas Becket.

Hinton St Mary, Dorset. The big tithe barn, built in the 15C was converted into a theatre and hall in c.1900 and 1929.

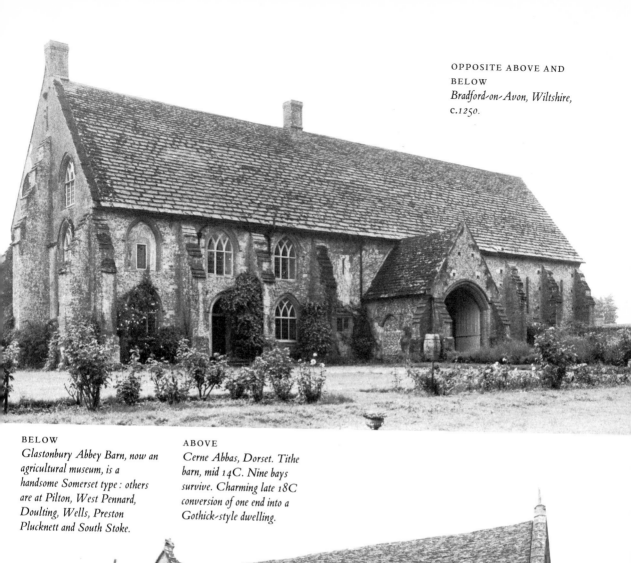

OPPOSITE ABOVE AND
BELOW
*Bradford-on-Avon, Wiltshire,
c.1250.*

BELOW

*Glastonbury Abbey Barn, now an
agricultural museum, is a
handsome Somerset type: others
are at Pilton, West Pennard,
Doulting, Wells, Preston
Plucknett and South Stoke.*

ABOVE

*Cerne Abbas, Dorset. Tithe
barn, mid 14C. Nine bays
survive. Charming late 18C
conversion of one end into a
Gothick-style dwelling.*

OPPOSITE ABOVE
Middle Littleton, Hereford and Worcester. National Trust, c.1220.

OPPOSITE BELOW
Ablington, Gloucestershire. Typical medieval Cotswold barn built when Cotswold wool dominated Europe.

Pilton, Somerset. One of a distinctive group around Glastonbury, c.1400. Only two or three barns in Britain are decorated with medallions of the Four Evangelists on the gables.

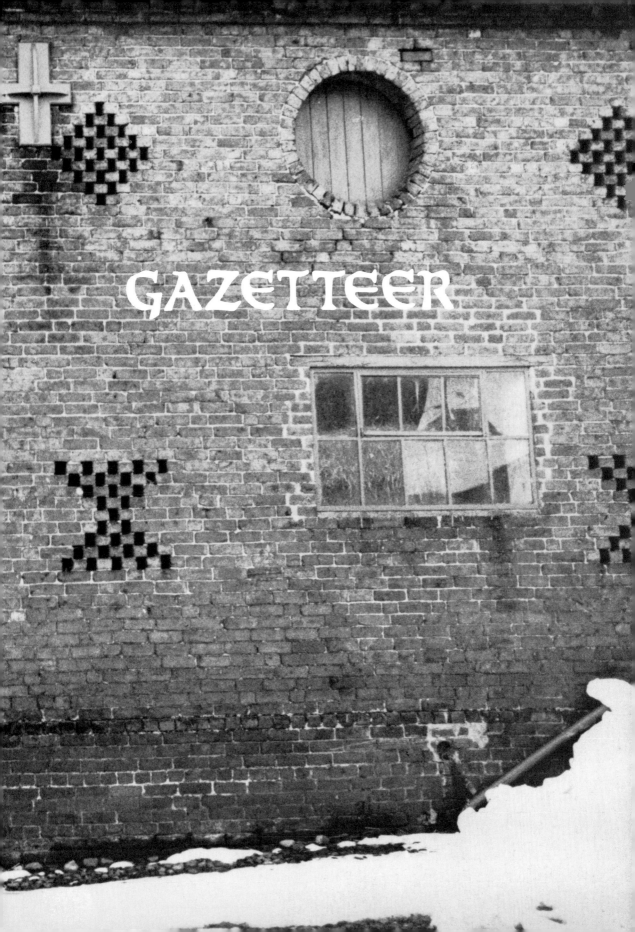

GAZETTEER

After the introductory paragraphs for each region – outstanding barns, and some which are ordinary but typical of their area, are listed in alphabetical order. Numbers in italic type following an entry indicate the page on which an illustration appears; other numbers refer to the pages on which the barn has been mentioned in the text.

Granite in the West
The Isles of Scilly, Cornwall and Devon

The flat, windswept Isles of Scilly, the hills of Cornwall with their remote, steep gullies and coombs, and the richer country of west Devon, all have one thing in common: hard grey granite. This local stone is the hardest in Britain, so when it was used for building it was often laid rough, without precise shaping either on its outside or round its edges. In the far West Country one expects to find the barns small and intimate, of no known date, and often with new roof timbers which suggest that the original roof interiors were rather poor: a reflection of the poverty of the farms. In the Isles of the Scilly, tiny stone sheds nestle against the slopes seemingly seeking shelter from the winter gales. The islands were more important in the sixteenth century, as a western strategic outpost, than they are today as a home of the nursery gardening industry for the daffodil. The population remained sparse until the arrival of the Dorrien-Smith family early in the nineteenth century, with their imaginative programme for agricultural development. The few barns which do exist on this island scene of heath, bracken and flowers, are probably no more ancient than the lighthouses, another product of nineteenth-century enterprise. The shape and appearance of the barns are more impressive than their age: the pink flecks in the granite walls, the thick layers of cement holding the big stones in place, the rounded corners streamlined against the wind, and the heavy deep-ridged tiles, all make a practical and satisfying impact on the eye.

Cornwall, like the Isles of Scilly, is an area of small hills unsuited to large-scale arable cultivation. So the

PREVIOUS PAGE
Typical Midlands 18C brick, with patterning. Between Alkington and Shawbury, Shropshire.

ABOVE
Typical of Cornwall and the Scillies. Above the harbour at Tresco, the Scilly Isles.

TOP

A typical farm group at Chapel Farm, Gooseham Mill, Morwenstow, Cornwall.

ABOVE

Styles of construction changed gradually; 15–16C stonework on the left, 13–14C on the right. West Chapple, Gidleigh, Devon.

barns are small, though numerous, and on open ground in the north. Some were probably built with the mining wealth accumulated by newly invented machinery in the late eighteenth century. The granite is often laid dry in horizontal slabs, almost without cement bonding, with roofs of slate from the local quarries. One of the typical farm villages hiding between the northern cliffs is Tregarthen, and there one

may count about four times as many barns – thirteen all told – as there are houses.

A characteristic Devon agricultural building (it is of course more than just a barn) is the long house which accommodated the people, livestock and produce under one roof. It often seems to have been built deliberately along a slope in order to help the drainage. Part of it was the cattle-shed. A long house was

Typical small Devon barn made of cob. Titchberry. National Trust.

early 1500s. Five-sided big blocks called snail's crawl, measuring up to 18 inches across, give walls a charming decorative pattern. This was especially popular in the eighteenth century, the age of superb finish.

Often blocks of granite were used as found, but when they were shaped the stone cutting was done by 'feather'. A hardwood wedge, which was inserted into a crack in the stone, swelled with the damp when water was poured into the cavity and caused the stone to crack. The men worked together with hammers and chisels, and sang a special song when the long crack developed. Mechanical jump drills are said to have been invented in 1814, and where they have been used they leave their traces in the form of a row of holes. At Powder Mills Farm on Dartmoor, such stones can be seen incomplete in the ground. Round marks therefore may indicate a working later than 1814.

In mid- and east Devon comes the ingenious, economical use of packed clay or mud and straw, sometimes with gravel, known as cob, which was built onto a stone foundation. A similar method is also found in Cambridgeshire, Wales and elsewhere.

frequently built in a barton or small farm. A good example is Chapple Farm near Gidleigh, where the granite long house was the home of no less than five families as recently as 1900. In 1980 it was restored, with another adjacent barn at West Chapple, helped by a grant from the local authority, and research there has thrown some light on the local techniques originally used to build barns.

Medieval barns in Devon sometimes had wooden steps leading to a loose first floor consisting simply of planks propped across the building on cantilevered stone stanchions. Later, spiral staircases were built over the edge of the fireplaces to let the heat upstairs. The type of stone walling helps to determine the date of the barn: an erratic long and short rhythm, horizontally, is a type of granite construction like a sort of organized rubble, and dates from the fourteenth or fifteenth century. Big rectangles, well-shaped though not accurately fitted, reflect the increased wealth of the

BROADHEMBURY, Devon. Kerswell Priory. Arch-brace roof, medieval wall paintings, probably a domestic monastic building. Future was in question but saved by 1981 planning inquiry preservation decision, supported by SPAB.
BUCKLAND MONACHORUM, Devon. Buckland Abbey, *see* illustration in Medieval Section. 42, *109*, *110*
COMBETEIGNHEAD, Devon. Five-bay thatched Dutch barn and linhay.
COTEHELE, Cornwall. 15C, National Trust, stone, built after Battle of Bosworth 1485.
GIDLEIGH, Devon. Long house. *17*, *135*, *136*
HARTLAND, Devon. Near the present village of Stoke, medieval remains of Hartland Abbey. 48
KILLOW, near Truro, Cornwall. Medieval walls, granite below, brick above with mouldings over windows.
LEIGH, near Churchstowe, Devon. Remains of a grange of Buckfast Abbey. Impressive arcades; staircase.
MORWENSTOW, Cornwall. Typical farm group at Chapel Farm, Gooseham Mill. *135*
TITCHBERRY, Cornwall. Fine granite group with circular horse-gin. Small cob barn at East Titchberry, National Trust. *30*, *136*

TORQUAY, Devon. Torre Abbey *see* Medieval Section. *108*

TREDREA, Perranaworthal, Cornwall. One of Britain's largest barns, 4½ miles southwest of Truro.

TREGARTHEN, Cornwall. Thirteen barns in same small village. *31, 76–7, 135*

TREMEDDA, Cornwall. 1926 barn, designer George Kennedy. *22, 74, 78–9*

TRENTISHOE, Devon. Fine granite group of farm buildings and barn around church.

Golden and grey stone

Somerset, Dorset, Avon, Gloucestershire, the Cotswolds, Wiltshire, Oxfordshire and Northamptonshire

The appearance of barns is determined more by their geography than by their date: local building materials and agricultural practice influence the colour and size of farm buildings, more than any prevailing architectural fashion. Nowhere is this more true than in the fertile peaceful limestone regions of Oxfordshire and Gloucestershire. The barns are very numerous and beautiful, but we do not know when or for whom the majority of them was built.

In most of them, the roof rests on the walls, so there is no aisle and no elaborate wooden framework to support an aisle truss. The woodwork is usually too simple to give us those interesting clues contained in some of the big timber joints of the medieval giants.

In Somerset there is a greater variety of building stone, for instance, carboniferous limestone in the Mendip Hills, and sandstones in the Quantocks. The chief building materials, however, are the warm Ham Hill stone which was used for the barn at Preston Plucknett near Yeovil, and the cold precise grey-blue lias, whose hardness makes possible a splendid precision of laying, as at One Tree Farm near East Lambrook.

Both stones together may be seen used at their finest at Muchelney, a fascinating and well-documented settlement. A Benedictine monastery was established here by a King of Wessex, perhaps as early as the eighth century – the oldest religious foundation in the county apart from Glastonbury Abbey. Destroyed by the Danes, the Benedictines' house was refounded around AD 950. It never had more than twenty monks. A visitation dated 1335 rebukes these brethren for 'living too

well: they had costly utensils and ornate beds, dined in private, rode about the country, kept unfit company and left the church in disrepair.' Today, much of the abbey's stone can be seen reused in the handsome surrounding eighteenth- and nineteenth-century farm buildings and barns, sometimes with the sophisticated horizontal stripes of different sorts of stone which are characteristic of Somerset.

In 1979/80 one of the most remote and beautiful English villages was the scene of an unexpected jousting match. At East Luccombe also in Somerset two of the 'knights in armour' were locked in seemingly mortal, if chivalrous, combat over the red-sandstone buildings which dominate the scene under the willow trees at the bend in the river. The farmer tenant of the National Trust said, 'I can't use my barns, they're too small and access to them is too crooked.' He asked permission to demolish them and build new barns in corrugated iron and asbestos instead. The National Trust surprisingly supported him at the local enquiry. Not so the small but William Morris-inspired Society for the Protection of Ancient Buildings, who bravely challenged the National Trust, the biggest power in the game, and won. The Newsletter of the Society for June 1979 records that its representative at the enquiry was at pains to point out the generally good working relationship between the Trust and the Society. 'We were most surprised to learn that the National Trust are the applicants. The barn is an unaltered example of a local type and is in a very prominent position within the village. The loss would be most regrettable and its replacement by a large modern Span farm building would do great harm to the village scene. . .'

The enquiry's finding was referred to the Secretary of State for the Environment. Happily, the final decision was against the application to demolish and the tenant farmer is finding that his old barns are after all usable as well as beautiful.

In Gloucestershire, the colour of the local Cotswold stone, as at Stanway, can only be described as honeyed. It is sometimes observed that Kent and Essex are the major barn counties, containing more and larger and less-altered specimens of these inert giant buildings. But the Cotswolds are supreme, if not in numbers, then in the most important matters of harmony and colour. Here, there are some of the great monuments of Europe disguised as humble farmsteads.

There are exceptional early medieval barns in this neighbourhood – Ashleworth, Bredon, Bretforton, Frocester, Hartpury, Middle Littleton, Siddington.

Another group of barns c.1400 near Glastonbury includes Doulting, Pilton, South Stoke, Wells, West Pennard, Westwood.

The great barn at Avebury can be dated from a careful reading of the antiquary William Stukeley's book on Avebury published in 1743. He showed in his engravings the prehistoric stone circle with the barn and its stone-built south wing where a bank had been removed. He says Lord Stowell, Lord of the Manor, 'Levell'd the vallum on that side of the town next to the church where the barn now stands.' As Lord Stowell was given his peerage in 1683, and sold the Manor House to Lord Holford in 1696, the barn must have been built between these dates, in about 1690.

It is 140 feet long by 36 feet wide, has nine bays with a hip bay at either end supported by a central half-cruck. It is surprisingly heavy and elaborate in construction for its date: the main timbers are as massive as they would have been in medieval times, although they are not as long, and the curves on some of the braces give them a Gothic flavour. This is perhaps the biggest and most impressive of all the barns listed in the Gazetteer that have been given a new use as a home for local agricultural bygones.

Barns throughout this great swathe of central England may be located partly by the colour of their stone: Shroton, near Blandford in Dorset, is a magnificent grey-stone thatched group in a farmyard with the church nearby. Tisbury is an even more ambitious, still almost complete monastic group of similar grey colour. Still in grey, Toller Fratrum has a medieval manor and hall beside its hilltop church and barn in remotest Dorset. Through the honey-coloured Cotswolds one reaches to the north the gold of Northamptonshire; there, at Passenham are two barns, fine examples of both their colour and date. They are at right angles to each other, one 110 feet long with a high roof and three collars, the other dated 1626.

ABBOTSBURY, Dorset. Abbotsbury Abbey Great Barn, built c.1400. Northeast part now ruined. Originally 276 × 31 feet; had stone-slab roof but is now thatched. 54, 106–7, 117
ABLINGTON, Gloucestershire. Medieval, date-stone 1727. See illustration in Medieval Section 13, 15, 130
AFFPUDDLE, Dorset. Seven barns, all similar and near each other, four of them differing by no more than 5 in. in their main measurements. Two are

recorded as being built in 1802. One has a brick mid-19C granary nearby.
ALDBOURNE, near Ramsbury, Wiltshire. Built in 1979 of austere traditional materials.
APETHORPE, near Oundle, Northamptonshire. Barn converted into the King's Head public house.
ASHLEWORTH, Gloucestershire. See illustration in Medieval Section. 116, 137
AVEBURY, Wiltshire. Big, thatched, agricultural museum. 34, 35, 82, 138
BARRINGTON COURT, Somerset. Designers Forbes and Tait, c.1920.
BATH, Avon. Bath University Arts Barn. Used for university arts events.
BEER, Gloucestershire. Good 19C group. 111
BIBURY, Gloucestershire. Good conversion with huge windows in the massive porch. 38
BISHOPS CLEEVE, Gloucestershire. 13C tithe barn. Truncated, now the village hall.
BRADFORD-ON-AVON, Wiltshire. Big medieval, stone. See illustration in Medieval Section. 109, 128
BRETFORTON, near Evesham, Gloucestershire. See illustration in Medieval Section. 120–1, 137
BRIDEHEAD, Dorset. Good Victorian group. Architect Benjamin Ferry. 74
BRYMPTON D'EVERCY, Somerset. Country museum. 39
BURFORD, Gloucestershire. Cotswold Folk Museum. 38
BURY BARN, Oxfordshire. Now used as a restaurant at the junction of the A40 and the Burford Link Road. Unrefined large-scale conversion.
CERNE ABBAS, Dorset. See illustration in Medieval Section. 129
CHILCOMBE, near Bridport, Dorset. Thatched barn with stone floor, used for making cider. Demolished by farmer in 1939 and replaced by new metal structure. Village, almost deserted since the Black Death in 1348, now consists of a small square formed of barns. The Victorian barn was a grain store and is now the studio of the painter John Hubbard.

OPPOSITE ABOVE
Typical medieval Dorset barn at Shroton.

OPPOSITE BELOW
Early wagon shed/Dutch barn; the barn behind is probably 18C. Shroton, Dorset.

Striped flint and brick, 18C. Fosbury, Wiltshire.

CHURCH ENSTONE, Oxfordshire. Datestone 1382. 69

CULHAM, near Henley-on-Thames, Oxfordshire. Fine chequered end to 14C barn, squares of clunch and flint. 145

CULHAM, near Abingdon, Oxfordshire. Bookshop belonging to Colin Franklin, antiquarian books scholar. Good conversion to library.

CUTSDEAN, Gloucestershire. Beautiful rural group, now derelict because planning permission refused. 83–4

DALLINGTON, Northamptonshire. By the Wheatsheaf public house.

DORCHESTER, Dorset. The Dorset County Museum. 39

DOULTING, Somerset. See illustration in Medieval Section. 123, 138

DRAYTON, Oxfordshire. Drastic conversion of mid-19C barn and long cowshed. Designed by the Parallel Lines group.

EAST LAMBROOK, Somerset. Early Dutch hay barn 22, 137

EASTLEACH, Gloucestershire. Sheepbridge Hill Barn has a Roman colonnade along the lower side of a beautiful sloping garden, edging the open cow byre which is now the covered entrance. Big uncluttered room, fireplace each end. Occasional concerts. Converted by Sir Guy Holland, MP.

EAST LUCCOMBE, Somerset. National Trust contemplated demolition. 137

EASTON GREY, near Malmesbury, Wiltshire. Whatley Manor, exceptional long barn at 115 ft.

EAST TYTHERTON, Wiltshire. Brick granary c.1810.

FIFIELD, near Burford, Oxfordshire. Good medium-sized barn conversion. 95–6, *97*, 100, 105

FOSBURY, Wiltshire. Flint and brick patterning. *140*, 145

FOXLEY, near Malmesbury, Wiltshire. A 1983 conversion of stone 18C barn with adjacent Tudor threshing barn.

FRAMPTON-UPON-SEVERN, Gloucestershire. Timber frame with wattle panels.

FROCESTER, Gloucestershire. See illustration in Medieval Section. *56, 57, 111, 137*

GLASTONBURY, Somerset. See illustration in Medieval Section and back of jacket. *36, 37, 129, 138*

GRAFTON ESTATE, Northamptonshire. Several farm barns built in the 1840s.

GREAT COXWELL, near Faringdon, Oxford-shire. A 13C emporium brought revenue to the Cistercian monks at Beaulieu Abbey. William Morris called it 'as noble as a cathedral'. *42, 45, 47, 52, 67, 110–11*

HARTPURY, Gloucestershire. Magnificent medieval stonework. Fine recent restoration jointly funded by local authority and farmer/owner. *13, 137*

HASELEY, Oxfordshire. Aisled tithe barn, arched wind braces *c.*1400. Seven bays, originally fourteen.

HIGHLEADON, Gloucestershire. Pierced brick nogging.

HILL DEVERIL, Devizes, Wiltshire. Tree trunks support the long medieval roof. Cromwell's soldiers slept here and used it to stable their horses. Today it is used for wedding receptions and barn dances.

HINTON ST MARY, Dorset. Ancestral home of Lord Rivers, now the home of Anthony Pitt-Rivers. In the 1850s his family developed a system of batch production of barns of uniform design, three of which are in Hinton. The ownership of a village by the Pitt family may often be indicated, according to Anthony Pitt-Rivers, by the presence of one of these barns. In the manor garden is a large 15C tithe barn by the church. It was converted to a hall before 1900 and to a theatre in 1929. Contains a huge 15C fireplace from Cerne Abbey installed in the 19C. *126–7*

HINTON WALDRIST, near Faringdon, Oxfordshire. A grange and two barns cleaned by Anthony Davenport, an antique dealer, who uses them as showrooms.

IWERNE COURTNEY *see* Shroton

KELMSCOTT MANOR, Oxfordshire. William Morris' home. *19, 110*

KINGSBURY EPISCOPI, Somerset. Burrow Hill Farm barn wall incorporates medieval stone lions from Muchelney. *47*

LACOCK ABBEY, Wiltshire. National Trust Fox Talbot photography museum in converted 17C barn. *141*

Lacock Abbey, Wiltshire. Well converted by National Trust into Fox Talbot photography museum — outside (above right) and inside (right).

MACARONI FARM, near Northleach, Gloucestershire. Good group with typical local overhanging lip on porches. *143*

MAIDEN NEWTON, Dorset. Correspondence of church and barn. *143*

MALMESBURY, Wiltshire. The Athelstan Museum. 38

MAPPERTON, Dorset. Fine manor complex.

MARSHFIELD, Avon. Castle Farm Museum. 38

MUCHELNEY, Somerset. Lias stone, Abbey decorated with lions, some removed. 47, *49*, 137

NEWENT, Gloucestershire. Large barn. Home and studio of Pauline Solven, glassblower, and of Cowdy Glass.

OXFORD, Oxfordshire. New College, Warden's Barn 1402, now part of College accommodation. Fine exterior. Original roof with king posts.

PASSENHAM, Northamptonshire. Two barns at right angles, datestone 1626. 72, 138

PILTON, Somerset. *See* illustration in Medieval Section. *131*, 138

POTTERSPURY, near Towcester, Northamptonshire. Conversion to Rudolph Steiner School.

POYNTINGTON, near Sherborne, Dorset. Good conversion.

PRESTON PLUCKNETT, near Yeovil, Somerset. *See* illustration in Medieval Section. *117*, 137

SEZINCOTE, Gloucestershire. Indian 'Hindu' style. 74, 150

SHIPTON-UNDER-WYCHWOOD, Oxfordshire. At Old Prebendal House there is a 15C tithe barn now redundant. Threat of demolition.

SHROTON (Iwerne Courtney), near Blandford, Dorset. Classic farmyard group. Great U-shaped thatched barn, with many dates scratched in clunch of interior walls, the earliest 1731. Perhaps 18C roof though walls look medieval. Also a 17C rectangular pigeon house and late 15C arcaded granary nearby with Dutch barn/wagon shed. 138, *139*

SIDDINGTON, Gloucestershire. *See* illustrations in Medieval Section. *120–1*, 137

SILVERSTONE, Northamptonshire. Rookery Farm Barns. The County Council threatens to demolish them for access to new housing, although the barns are still in use. Unassuming, solid vernacular, *c.*18C.

SOUTHMOOR, near Abingdon, Oxfordshire. At Court Close there is a rare classical barn, *c.*1640.

SOUTH STOKE, near Bath, Avon. Fine medieval group, barn and dovecot combined. Restored in 1930s. *28–9*, 138

STANTON, Gloucestershire. Typical tithe barn near church. 14C. *8–9*

STANWAY, Gloucestershire. Field Barn. Marvellous, isolated site beside a cottage. Converted by architect Jeremy Benson, Vice-Chairman of SPAB. New roof inside and out, new timbers, large chimneys, huge interior room. 137, *144*

STOKE-SUB-HAMDON, near Yeovil, Somerset. Good thatched stone group. National Trust. *See* illustration in Medieval Section. *123*

SYDLING ST NICHOLAS, Dorset. Tithe barn with nine and half bays. Initials of Ursula Walsingham, widow of Elizabeth I's principal secretary, inscribed. Corrugated iron roof.

TAINTON, near Highnam, Gloucestershire. Unusual undercroft.

TARRANT MONKTON, Dorset. Good conversion, shown in Royal Academy 1981 by Robert Martin.

TAYNTON, near Burford, Oxfordshire. Two enormous barns converted very well 1980–83. One room 52 ft long. Secluded site by River Windrush.

TEMPLE GUITING, near Stow-on-the-Wold, Gloucestershire. Sympathetic conversion. *90–1*, *102–3*, *102–4*

THAME, Oxfordshire. In Church Road, a very large 16C brick half-timbered three-storey tithe barn by the church, used for storing books. Fine exterior, almost unaltered. 42

THORPE WATERVILLE, Northamptonshire. Church Farm. Chimney, chamfered windows, possibly incorporating fragments of masonry from the nearby fortified manor.

TISBURY, Wiltshire. Spendid group, one of the longest medieval barns *c.*200 ft. Stone walls, 13 bays, 2 tiers of collar beams, the lower with arched braces; 3 tiers of wind braces. Alec Clifton-Taylor, historian, calculates there are 1,450 square yds of thatching. The whole Place Farm complex was part of the grange of

OPPOSITE ABOVE
Regional peculiarities intrigue the connoisseur : Cotswold porches often have a lip over the gable door. Macaroni Farm, near Northleach, Gloucestershire.

OPPOSITE BELOW
Typical small medieval barn built by its church. Maiden Newton, Dorset.

Field Barn, Stanway, Gloucestershire. Conversion by architect-owner Jeremy Benson.

the nunnery of Shaftesbury. *See* illustration in Medieval Section. *66*, 115, *116*, 138

TOLLER FRATRUM, Dorset. Fine group with granary. 115, 138

TOLPUDDLE, Dorset. Martyrs met in barn.

ULEY COMMON, near Dursley, Gloucestershire. Big L-shaped barn in classic situation at the heart of the village.

UPPER HEYFORD, Oxfordshire. Near the Oxford Canal. A masterpiece of *c.*1400 built for William of Wykeham. Compare Harmondsworth in Greater London.

WATCHET, near Taunton, Somerset. Fine arcade ground floor, big room above.

WELLS, Somerset. *See* illustration in Medieval Section. *125*, 138. Also ruins of 12C Canons' Barn.

WEST CHALDON FARM, near Dorchester, Dorset. Two barns in continuous range. Brick, about 150 ft long. Thatched, original corn bins inside, early 18C.

WEST DEAN, Wiltshire. Church Farmhouse. Brick buttressed, 13-bay barn.

WEST KNIGHTON, near Dorchester, Dorset. Handsome brick, unusual for Dorset. Datestone 1704; despite late date, the buttresses are in Gothic style.

WESTONBIRT, Gloucestershire. Good Victorian model farm 74, *78*, 111.

WEST PENNARD, Somerset. *See* illustration in Medieval Section. 19, *20*, 138

WESTWOOD, Wiltshire. 15C stone barn east of the church. 138

WINCHCOMBE, Gloucestershire. Big medieval tithe barn.

WOODSPRING PRIORY, Avon. *See* illustration in Medieval Section. *126–7*

WOODSTOCK, Oxfordshire. Oxfordshire County Museum, at Fletcher's House. 39

WYKE, near Sherborne, Dorset. Two barns in continuous range. About 230 ft long, buttressed walls, collar beams and curved wind braces in fine roofs.

Flint on the Downs
West and East Sussex

Flint creeps into buildings with brick in patches along the Berkshire Downs. Near Hungerford, at Fosbury in Wiltshire, it appears in typically eighteenth-century strips; at Culham near Henley-on-Thames, in fourteenth-century chequerboard with chalk; at Harting in West Sussex in brilliant eighteenth-century solid chalk patches (clunch) which make a marvellous random impact; at Billingshurst flint provides a good emphatic foil to the soft colours and contours of the brown West Sussex stone. But flint becomes dazzling and almost universal going east from Chichester. Sometimes, as at Wyatt's big house at West Dean College, or at nearby Goodwood, or at Firle Place to the east, near Glyndebourne, the flint is knapped into pleasing, tight-fitting rectangles almost like bricks, glistening black with an elegant, narrow white surround. But unlike brick this is only a facing, each flint being usually only $1\frac{1}{2}$ inches thick. These great houses also have smart flint-knapped farm buildings, but more like stables than barns. Flint for barns was usually left natural, speckled grey, white and black, and constructed with a sort of lime rubble down the centre to hold together the layers of flint back and front. The colour and composition of a flint wall compares well with many abstract paintings today, and the shape of the flint barns through East Sussex to Pevensey and beyond gives a unique and distinguished character to the generous bulge of the South Downs.

The mother of several of these barns was Michelham Priory. Built in the thirteenth and fourteenth centuries for the Augustinian canons, it was founded by Gilbert de l'Aigle, Lord of the Castle of Pevensey, who obtained permission from Henry III and gave lands in the region, as well as at Pevensey, Willingdon and Seaford to support the Priory. There seem never to have been more the twelve priests, who had dwindled to only eight and one novice at the Dissolution, when some of them found jobs as parish priests. The eighteen waiting servants and eleven 'hinds' or outdoor labourers must also have profited from and contributed to, local agriculture. The monastery buildings were mostly pulled down and the materials sold. The ruins were subsequently lived in by the great Sussex family of Pelham, then by the Sackvilles. In the mid-sixteenth century, the Great Barn was built of oak and elm, with a thatched roof which was replaced in 1970 with hand-made Sussex tiles. The flint and stone ends make a

pleasing contrast in colour. The rest of the buildings are of typical stone, Eastbourne greensand (a sort of sandstone), Sussex ironstone and Caen stone from France, brough up the River Cuckmere by boat, with chalk and flint found locally.

In a 6-mile area west of Beachy Head, round the Seven Sisters chalk cliffs, the Seven Sisters Country Park has mapped out no less than thirty barns worthy of a visit. The Park's information centre is itself in a fine eighteenth-century flint barn at Exceat on the River Cuckmere. Its neighbouring barns to which its exhibitions draw attention enjoy names like Plonk Barn, Comp Barn, Fox Hole Barn, Acorn Barn, Barley Barn, Hill Cottage Barn, Crapham Barn, Clapham Barn. But the most common name is New Barn — there are half a dozen of them, a hint at the prosperity brought by the new agriculture of the eighteenth century. One of the longest, a typical Sussex structure built in discreet flint, with ten bays, is New Barn, near Birling Gap, with attached outshot, cowshed or hovel. It is isolated and secluded, almost hidden under the hills, an ideal site for camping or caravans, but now emptied by agriculture and planners alike, waiting, like so many barns, to collapse, and to become a sad lament of our uncaring times.

The four biggest flint barns in the region are all sheltered under the Downs. They display the squat, gnarled look of the flint and are all partly buried under their surrounding chalky banks. They are all spacious, aisled structures, probably lower than most in relation to their great width, certainly with very small porches in relation to their great length.

Timber is less common in Sussex than elsewhere in the south. One of Sussex's biggest medieval barns, recently re-roofed. Court Farm Barn, Falmer, East Sussex.

Court Farm Barn at Falmer is the only one still thatched. Recently and splendidly restored, its peaceful position between Georgian farmhouse, village pond and open fields belies its closeness to the motorway and to Sussex University.

Better known and probably older is the greatest flint barn in Britain, at Alciston. Built by the monks of Battle Abbey 15 miles across the Downs, like Falmer, it is still in active use for farming. But Alciston is an altogether grander structure than Falmer with its L-shape, the longer leg being an impressive 170 feet, and with its large farmyard and fine seventeenth-century farmhouse and medieval dovecot. Indeed, the key to the beauty of Alciston is its whole environment, one of the most complete and unchanged farmsteads anywhere.

The third big flint barn is at Patcham near Brighton: it can claim more length than antiquity, and more splendours inside than out. It is 260 feet long, perhaps the longest in the whole of Britain, certainly in Sussex.

The fourth great flint manifestation is Charleston Manor, by Litlington, East Sussex, not to be confused with the country home of the Bloomsbury group at Charleston by Firle.

OPPOSITE ABOVE AND BELOW
Typical Sussex, mostly of flint. Alciston, one of Britain's biggest and finest medieval barns, East Sussex.

BELOW
At Charleston Manor, Litlington, East Sussex, one of the county's four big flint barns – the others are at Alciston, Falmer and Patcham.

BILLINGSHURST, West Sussex. Stone. Demolished for reuse of materials. *65*, 87, 145

BIRLING GAP, East Sussex. Birling Manor has the biggest group of barns in Sussex – six big flint buildings. New Barn nearby. 145

BISHOPSTONE, East Sussex. Four dwellings from barns and cowsheds in village centre. A second clutch of conversions adjoins the fields eastward, so the whole village centre is now used for dwellings in barns instead of for farm storage. 82

BURWASH, East Sussex. Watermill.

CHARLESTON MANOR *see* Litlington.

CHIDDINGLY, East Sussex. Elizabethan manor house, Place Farm, *c*.1500, part converted into a magnificent barn in the 16C and 18C. Finest quality. *149*

CHYNGTON, Seaford, East Sussex. Square flint dovecot, 600 nesting places in chalk interior. Possibly

Norman. Big barn group converted. Beggar's Barn on South Hill nearby.

EXCEAT, East Sussex. Seven Sisters Country Park. 36, *38–9*, 145

FALMER, East Sussex. Huge, thatched, medieval. *58*, 111, *145*, 147

FIRLE, East Sussex. Flint-knapping. 145

FOREST ROW, near East Grinstead, East Sussex. Old Surrey Hall. Romantic flowery surroundings.

GOODWOOD, West Sussex. Smart flintwork. 76, 145

GREAT DIXTER *see* Northiam.

HARTING, West Sussex. Clunch. 145

HERSTMONCEUX, East Sussex. Rare 15C brickwork.

HORAM, East Sussex. Typical 18C 47, *48*

HOVE, East Sussex. Barn, *c*.1820, windmill on top.

BELOW

Planning struggles won at Alfriston; Duke's Green Barn, simple conversion into a dwelling 1972. East Sussex.

OPPOSITE

Chiddingly, East Sussex. 15C brick, an exciting, original group, back (above) and front (below).

LITLINGTON, East Sussex. At Charleston Manor. Magnificent angled flint barn 177 ft long. Restored by Sir Oswald and Lady Birley in 1930s and used by them for theatrical performances, including the Russian Ballet. Circular medieval dovecot comparable to Dunster, Somerset. *66, 147*

LITTLEHAMPTON, West Sussex. At Rosemead School, Arts Barn.

MICHELHAM, East Sussex. Priory, great barn c.1600. Museum. 36, 105, 145

MILTON STREET, East Sussex. Datestone 1832. 74

NORTHEASE, Brakey Bottom, near Lewes, East Sussex. Occasional concerts – the audience sits on straw bales.

NORTHIAM, East Sussex. Great Dixter, good conversion by Lutyens of barn and outbuildings in outstanding garden. 79

PATCHAM, East Sussex. Possibly the longest barn in Britain, c.260 ft. Flint walls. 42, 147

ROTTINGDEAN, East Sussex. Bateman's, home of Rudyard Kipling 1902–36, built in 1634 by a local iron-master in the Weald where much of Britain's iron was smelted. Watermill grinds corn for National Trust visitors; beside is an early water-turbine engine, perhaps the world's oldest still in working order, installed by Kipling to generate electricity for his house. He was one of the National Trust's three founders. Acquired by the Trust in 1955 through the efforts of his daughter, Dorothy. Two-storey wooden barn converted to a base camp for volunteers working on nearby sites.

SEDLESCOMBE, Battle, East Sussex. Norton's Farm Museum. 36

SINGLETON, West Sussex. Weald and Downland Open Air Museum. 36, *120–1,* 150

STANMER, East Sussex. Horse gin. 29, 150

WESTDEAN, near Litlington, East Sussex. Three large tithe barns converted together, imaginative and modern in effect. Architect Wycliffe Stutchbury. A fourth, bigger barn is a drastic and imposing conversion.

WILMINGTON PRIORY, East Sussex. Agricultural Museum, 36, 82; Place Barn – good conversion. *100–1, 101–2,* 105

WISBOROUGH GREEN, West Sussex. Fine granary, half-timbered and brick.

Wood and brick in the Home Counties

Hampshire, Berkshire, Buckinghamshire, Bedfordshire, Surrey, Greater London and Hertfordshire

In the southern counties, almost all sorts of building materials were used for barns. Most common are the great timber-clad barns like those at Rogate, Sutton or Trotton.

A great arc of barns with internal timber frames and external weather-boarding curves north from Titchfield in Hampshire, through London, then south to the East Sussex/Kent border. Then the area of wood barns fans out into Kent and Essex.

Hampshire possesses a unique barn at Hockley Mill. It has datestones inscribed 1803, and in a way they should be called tombstones. For this type of building was made to house machines at the end of the eighteenth century. And it was these machines that sounded the death knell of the old threshing and storing processes in the barn.

This is almost a 'museum', showing the decline of the barn. The original threshing machine has vanished. To see a horse-driven 'gin' or circular gear to provide power for threshing or grinding, or for raising water from a well, one must visit Stanmer Park near Brighton, or the museum at Singleton in West Sussex. But at Hockley is a later successor dated 1880 – an iron water-wheel, 12 feet 6 inches in diameter with its huge wooden cog wheels, providing power for the threshing machine.

The barn at Old Ditcham Farm near Buriton, Petersfield, built of brick and flint in a massive Gothick style with a datestone 1758, is a solid monument, not the sort of folly usually associated with Gothick. Yet it is built in the most fashionable prevailing style of town dwelling, with no less than three pairs of doors down each side leading onto the farmyard. The stonework, exceptional for a barn, is not rough, but faced with a smooth ashlar surface in the manner usually reserved for the finer Georgian mansions. There are only two barns elsewhere in the country to compare with Old Ditcham. One is in the Indian style, at Sezincote in Gloucestershire, designed by S. P. Cockerell in about 1800. It is all stucco and show, all fantasy and fun, hardly tough enough in style to suggest its essential function. The other is at Marske in remote Swaledale, Yorkshire, possibly designed by John Carr of York in about 1795. It combines a

country solidity with elegant town grace in a way that is both impressive and incongruous. The Yorkshire stone is lighter in colour than the Hampshire, the Yorkshire mock-fortress outline is more amusing than the Hampshire, and the small Yorkshire Gothick window openings are more practical than the big windows and arches in Hampshire. But perhaps it is the Hampshire barn that lingers longest in memory: it is bigger, more serious and much earlier. Indeed it

RIGHT

Arched wind braces were a sophisticated provision hardly seen before 1400, to stop the rafters moving diagonally lengthwise, or 'raking'. Ridge beams along the top are rare in the south before the late 19C. Old Basing, Hampshire, c.1530.

was built only eight years after Horace Walpole began his life-long pastime in 1749 of creating Strawberry Hill, Europe's first 'Gothick' building, which he called his 'Little Gothic castle'. The Ditcham barn is unknown, whereas Strawberry Hill is world-famous, a reflection of the relative importance we place on buildings that are functional as opposed to artistic.

The king of the early brick barns is unquestionably the 'tithe' barn at Grange Farm, Old Basing, near Basingstoke. Now entirely surrounded by motorways and railways, its owner can no longer fill it with his produce, for he has none. However, he used the barn for a great medieval dinner and barn dance in 1979, to the delight of his neighbours. The building is not only an original and magnificent construction – it represents a model of modern community cooperation.

In early 1977 the roof tiling became dangerous, with some rotten battens and the possibility of the tiles sliding to the ground. The consequent retiling of the roof and repairs to some wood and brickwork cost £16,000: 60 per cent of this was paid by the Historic Buildings Council and the balance by Basingstoke and Deane Borough Councils and the Hampshire County Council.

At Peper Harow, near Milford and Godalming in Surrey, is a dignified and symmetrical granary complex built in warm eighteenth-century brick. Round the courtyard there are open-sided cowsheds or byres, enclosed threshing barns, cottages, and open-sided wagon sheds. In the middle is a large two-storey granary group with staddle stones and a charming exterior staircase. Below, between the columns is a wagon park; above, a granary big enough to supply an army. This granary is at least six times larger than one of the largest of similar type – the pyramid 'pepperpot' roof, brick-built granaries dated 1752, once at Little-hampton but now in the Weald and Downland Open Air Museum at Singleton. Peper Harow has three roof ridges, with original eighteenth-century tiles and pantiles, and to crown the pleasure of visiting the settlement, one may see there plenty of farm people and produce. This is the earthy English equivalent of the more artificial Marie Antoinette's *Hameau* at Versailles. Peper Harow Farm was built no doubt as part of the walled garden and model estate of the neighbouring mansion, Peper Harow Park, home of Lord Middleton, now a secluded school.

There is an amazing contrast offered by the runways and the screaming jet engines at London Airport, Heathrow, on the one hand, and the fine medieval tithe barn, 190 feet long, still in farm use at Harmondsworth, on the other – an almost irreconcilable clash, as the new airborne life shatters the old on the land. The roof timbers inside are exceptionally fine and well-preserved, and some of the vertical, tarred wood-plank cladding outside seems to be original too. Built possibly for William of Wykeham in about 1390, it was like

Upper Heyford, Oxfordshire the property of Winchester Cathedral.

Another good early survivor is the timber tithe barn at Headstone Lane originally attached to Headstone Manor, in Pinner Park, near Harrow, now rather spoiled but fulfilling a useful function as a hall for occasional concerts and assemblies.

These two buildings make a good epilogue to the saga of the overcrowded capital city's impact on its neighbouring agricultural land. Many fine barns are still in use, maintaining an anachronistic way of life which is going to come under increasing threat as agriculture becomes more intensive; many more must be converted to new uses if the countryside is to avoid irreparable loss.

ANDOVER, Hampshire, Weyhill Wildlife Park and Rural Life Museum. 39.

ASHTEAD, Surrey. Three tiers – the top one for hay and stores, the middle one for winter feed, and the bottom tier for animals. Common type in bank barns of the Lake District and field barns of the Yorkshire Dales.

ASTON BURY MANOR, near Stevenage, Hertfordshire. Tudor, Grade I barn with another fine barn nearby.

ATTIMORE, Welwyn Garden City, Hertfordshire. Barns arts shop.

AYOT ST LAWRENCE, Hertfordshire. Bride Hall has two fine Elizabethan barns, one on each side of the big house forming an imposing U-shape.

BARKWAY, near Royston, Hertfordshire. Timber-framed and clad tithe barn.

BEAULIEU, Hampshire. Important medieval remains of Abbey which owned St Leonard's barn. 56, 110

BISHAM ABBEY, near Marlow, Buckinghamshire. Grange barns well converted. Pyramidal house at end of big aisled barn.

BRADWELL ABBEY, Buckinghamshire. Cruck blade remains.

BREAMORE, Hampshire. Agricultural museum. 36

BROUGHTON, Stockbridge, Hampshire. Buildings near Manor Farm. Renovated 18C barn in isolated, commanding position on chalk downs.

BURITON, Hampshire. Historic tithe barn, clunch. 115

BURNHAM ABBEY, near Dorney Green, Berkshire. Double tie beam like Bredon. Medieval barn converted in 1930.

BURSLEDON, Hampshire. Now a public house.

BYNSFIELD, Hampshire. Used for the children's television series 'Wurzel Gummidge'.

CHALFONT ST GILES, Buckinghamshire. Chiltern Open Air Museum. 36

CHESHAM BOIS, Buckinghamshire. Manor Barn 1607. Tithe barn and other barns adjacent.

COMPTON, Hampshire. Parsonage farm barn 1781, drastic conversion.

DITCHAM near Petersfield, Hampshire. Gothic revival. 150, 151

DUNSFOLD, near Guildford, Surrey. Bourne Hall Tudor barn from Wherstead. Grade II, re-erected by Preservation in Action, a building firm from Diss. Negotiations took nine months, the building six.

Big porches are typical of the Chilterns, not of Sussex where the high winds might make the porches too vulnerable. Fingest, Buckinghamshire.

EAST HENDRED, Berkshire. Good conversion of thatched barn. Architect Irene Mardl.

EDLESBOROUGH, Buckinghamshire. Church Farm Barn, brick nogging. 158

ELTHAM, London SE9. In Well Hall Road is Tudor Barn Art Gallery. More impressive outside than in. Also Great Hall finished *c.*1479, about 100 × 36ft, 6 bays, one of the finest medieval timber roofs in Britain, hammer beams with moulded main timbers, four-centred braces, varying in direction from apex to ridge. Built as part of Edward IV's moated royal palace, but used as a barn for several centuries, and shown as such in old prints. Big barn door in one side is a later addition for agricultural use. 157

FINGEST, Buckinghamshire. Fine brick and flint. *154*

GUILDFORD, Surrey. Wanborough Manor Farm.

HADDENHAM, Buckinghamshire. Large 15C near church and Manor Farmhouse. Six bays, aisles, tie beams on braces, diagonal queen posts. 158

HARMONDSWORTH, Greater London. Near London Airport, Heathrow. *See* illustration in Medieval Section. *51, 52, 152, 157*

HARTLEY WINTNEY, Hampshire. Conversion by Schultz Weir, with Arts and Crafts movement furniture inside by the Barnsley family and by Gimson.

HEADSTONE MANOR *see* Pinner.

HILLINGDON, Greater London. Farm Museum to which a 16C Grade II tiled barn is being moved by the GLC from Brockley Hill near Stanmore, where London Transport own the ground and refuse to restore the barn.

HITCHAM, Buckinghamshire. Belongs to the Hanbury family; proposed improvements caused village outcry.

HOCKLEY MILL, Hampshire. Datestone 1803, early mechanization. 150

HOOK, Hampshire. Granary.

HORSENDEN, near Princes Risborough, Buckinghamshire. Occasional concerts.

HUNGERFORD, Berkshire. Folly Farm. Granary, threshing floor. *13, 154-5*

ABOVE AND OPPOSITE
Folly Farm, Hungerford, Berkshire. Good modern conversion of typical Berkshire barn, by Mrs Amabel Lindsay.

JORDANS, Buckinghamshire. Quaker village. 'Mayflower' barn using some of pilgrim ship's 17C timber.

KNEBWORTH, Hertfordshire. Home of Bulwer-Lyttons. Recent unique removal operation of two barns which have been resited and preserved for tourist use. Conversion by Donald Insall. *80–81, 87*

LITTLE BEDWYN, Hampshire. Beautiful 18C brick farmyard, big barn porches. *14, 115*

LITTLE BERKHAMPSTEAD, Hertfordshire. Lavish conversion incorporating great walls, marble floor. William Tatton-Brown, architect, once partner in Tecton group, one of Europe's pioneers of modern architecture in the 1930s. Stylish and luxurious.

LOUDWATER, Buckinghamshire. Holtspur Bottom Farm between Beaconsfield and High Wycombe. Two good conversions.

MIDDLINGTON, Hampshire. Good early 19C model farm layout. Flint and brick, crisp outlines. Datestone 1848.

MONKEN HADLEY, Greater London. Tithe barn.

MUNSTEAD WOOD, Surrey. Lutyens' work. *79*

NEWBURY, Berkshire. Agricultural museum. *38*

OLD BASING, near Basingstoke, Hampshire. Grange Farm. Fine brickwork, probably 16C, 120 ft by 28 ft, two tiers of 'oilets' or ventilation slots. *2–3, 42, 152–3*

OLD BURSLEDON, Hungerford Bottom, Hampshire. Lone Barn. Medieval oak frame moved from the downs above Winchester, now a museum of agricultural bygones. Edward III's order of 1338 punishing malefactors who illegally cut trees dem-

Rogate, Hampshire. Exceptionally thick thatch, big porch.

onstrates the importance of local oak trees for building and for ships. Some 3700 loads of oak were needed to build a 64-gun ship.

OVINGTON, Hampshire. Diaper pattern on walls, dated 1872.

PEPER HAROW, Godalming, Surrey. Granary c.1600. Twenty-five timber supports. Fine brick barn complex. 152.

PINNER, Greater London, Headstone Manor, Headstone Lane. Big tithe barn near the station. Used for concerts and meetings. Now also a museum belonging to Havering Borough. Remnants of 15C house, c.1600 tiled roof; queen posts. 153

RAMSDELL, near Basingstoke, Hampshire. Ramsdell Ham Farmhouse – Nigel Sweetings' Barn Gallery.

READING, Berkshire. Museum of English Rural Life. 39

ROGATE, Hampshire. Typical timber cladding and characteristic huge thatched porches. 53, 150, 156

ROMSEY, Hampshire. Moor Court. Datestone 1701.

RUISLIP, Greater London. Great Barn before 1324. Good timbers. A second big barn is the public library with roof c.1600 and bowling green outside, opened 1937. Both given to the local authority by King's College, Cambridge.

ST LEONARD'S, Hampshire. Medieval ruins. Two big end walls of Beaulieu Abbey's barn. (See under Horn in Bibliography.)

SELBORNE, Hampshire. Gilbert White's home.

SLYFIELD, near Leatherhead, Surrey. Huge red-brick, spendid concert barn, used by Menuhin School. Fine gardens. Converted excellently by Sir Roland Harris.

STOCKBRIDGE, Hampshire. Lutyens' design at Marsh Court. 79

TITCHFIELD ABBEY, Hampshire. Big, medieval; wall and roof patterns. 150 by 37 ft. Probably built before 1400, one of the finest medieval barns in the country; some rebuilding 13, 69, 151

TROTTON, Hampshire. Typical timber cladding. 150

TWYFORD, Hampshire. Manor Farm. Reuse of monastic stones. 48

UPMINSTER, Greater London. Hall Barn in Hall Lane. Within walking distance of the Metropolitan Underground station. With Eltham, Ruislip, and Harmondsworth, one of the finest medieval barns in the Greater London area. Now a folk, agricultural and local history museum. Weather-boarded, thatched roof, aisled, with crown posts, four bays either side of central midstrey. The scarf-joints are edge-halved and bridle-butted with four face pegs and two edge pegs. Probably mid-15C. New College Oxford was the big local landowner. Scheduled Ancient Monument. 36

UPPER WINCHENDEN, Buckinghamshire. On road from Long Crendon to Waddesdon. Group of minor barns well converted.

WANTAGE, Berkshire. Lains Barn, 18 or 19C converted for public use by Dr Squires, local barn lover. 13, 57, 68, 83, 87

WELL END, Hampshire. Modern, soft wood needs iron bolts to stabilize.

WELWYN GARDEN CITY, Hertfordshire. In Handside Lane is a Barn Theatre. Probably c.17C. Converted c.1950.

WEST MEON, Hampshire. Barn repaired by owner/farmer. 24–5

WESTONING, Bedfordshire. Dashing conversion of half-timbered barn to house for twelve handicapped children and three staff. Architect Theo Crosby.

WINSLOW, Buckinghamshire. In Horn Street. This barn has a dwelling at one end, and at the other end is Paul Millichip's artist's studio. It is a sensitive conversion of a large 18C brick complex.

The soft barns of wood, and wattle and daub
Kent and Essex

Kent is often called the Garden of England because of its flowering fruit trees and its intensive cultivation. It was here that a special type of storage building, similar to a barn, was invented, to fulfil a special purpose. This was the oasthouse for the drying and preparation of hops, a local crop grown for brewing beer. The main characteristic of the oast, its square tower, is one which Kent shares with Hereford and Worcester; it seems, however, to have yielded, around 1800 in Kent, to the charming round cone with its big wind vanes. The round tower at Brook, across the lawn from the barn of c.1300 at Wye College Museum may be the earliest in the county, with a datestone of 1815. A good group of square towers and barns of similar date is owned by the National Trust at Outridge Farm, Toys Hill, Kent.

Oasts were a basic part of the beer production cycle: they were for beer what barns were, indirectly, for the production of bread. Oasts, like barns, have been parted from their original functions by new technology. But oasts were so common, and beer in such demand, that sometimes they invaded their bigger, rougher neighbours – the barns. For instance, the thirteenth-century barn at Boxley was used partly as an oasthouse in the eighteenth and nineteenth centuries – one can see that this was so from the tell-tale chimney in the middle of one side, and the interior shelving and compartments. Several smaller barns have incorporated oasts at one end.

The bigger Kent barns are in the arable region known as Old Kent, where the rich religious foundations could spread themselves. The neighbouring Weald had smaller tenures and a mixed economy including hop fields and fruit orchards which resulted in the building of smaller barns that are more varied and less glorious. But the medieval Kentish barn tends to be of similar construction throughout the county, and recent researches indicate an early medieval date for a surprisingly large proportion of the survivors.

Most early Kent barns are aisled with two rows of big timber posts to support the roof. What distinguishes them is the way in which the posts have a diagonal wooden buttress, sometimes called a shore, descending outwards from the top of the post to the bottom of the outside wall, resting usually not in the wall or the ground but in a plate or beam running along the ground. Half-way down, this shore meets a small horizontal tie beam leading outwards from the posts to the outer wall, and they slot into each other.

These Kent barns resemble somewhat the early Chiltern aisled barns like Edlesborough or Haddenham.

If Kent is an enormous garden, Essex is England's farmyard. Wherever you look in this rustic area, you see arable land and barns, crops and farmers. The landscape is not so much punctuated by its barns, as made by them. Essex, unlike Kent, has very little building stone in the soil, so its barn walls are usually built of clay with weather-board or clapboard. The half-timber construction, muted beige in colour, soft in outline, irregular in its grid, is indeed almost like a farm in its need for constant renewal.

Timber barns are as numerous and as early as those in Kent, and probably larger on average, but with more varied construction. A common distinguishing feature is that their shores extend not from the top of

the principal post to ground level as in Kent, but only half way down, to the point of junction of the lateral brace (aisle tie beam) with the outside wall.

The building of Essex barns shows a constancy over the centuries: change in this area seems to have been slower than elsewhere. The aisled barn, for instance, became rare in the south after the Middle Ages, but in Essex, (and in some other regions like Buckinghamshire) aisles remained normal.

Another aspect of this constancy of tradition extends into our present age. It is thatching. Nowhere else is thatch still so commonly used. There may be thirty thatchers still at work in Essex: Norman Scarfe, the East Anglian architectural historian, notes with admiration the Shelley family from Hockley who, father, son and grandson, may all work together on the same roof.

dismantled 1965 for new houses, now diminished and rebuilt.

FAIRSTEAD, Essex. Aisled, medieval.

FARNINGHAM, Kent. Roman masonry in walls and floor, Britain's best colour-tiled medieval roof. 67

FELSTEAD, Essex. Aisled.

FRINDSBURY, Isle of Corn, Kent. 210 ft. Finest medieval barn interior in Kent, 13 bays. *50, 52, 63*

GREAT DUNMOW, Essex. At Parsonage Farm, 17C with two big porches, major conversion in 1979.

HADLOW, near Tonbridge, Kent. Large 18C in centre of a group with six round oast houses at each corner. Radical conversion but still impressive.

HATFIELD BROAD OAK, Essex. Conversion by architectural group. *96, 98, 100, 103*

INGATESTONE HALL, Essex. Large brick, big buttresses, stepped gables, *c.1500*.

LAYER MARNEY, Colchester, Essex. Large barn, mostly timber. Like the adjoining hall finished in *c.1525*, very sophisticated. Brick for lower walls probably made from clay quarried from the neighbouring pond.

LENHAM, Kent. Giant thatched medieval masterpiece by the church.

LITTLEBOURNE, Kent, one of the barns of St Augustine's Abbey, Canterbury, is, with seven full bays, shorter at 172 ft long, and wider than Frindsbury; has a thatched roof. Original single entry changed to two. Perhaps built just after 1300, half a century later than Frindsbury. *52*

MAIDSTONE, Kent. Barn now used as coach museum, originally part of medieval archbishop's palace. Called 'Archbishop's stables'.

MANUDEN, Essex. Tithe barn, pink plaster on brick and flint base.

ST OSYTH'S PRIORY, Essex. Large 16C, by gatehouse. Stone one side, others timber-framed.

Once thought to be the oldest barn in Britain. Only three ruined 13C bays survived after decades of decay and indecision: Grange Barn, Coggeshall, Essex. Restoration has now been completed.

ABOVE
*Beautiful early 16C brickwork at Sturry, Kent; belonged to the
Augustinian Abbey of Canterbury.*

LEFT
*Typical of Essex with three threshing porches, timber and plaster
construction, low-lying. Wendens Ambo, near Saffron Walden.*

OPPOSITE
*One of the longest barn repair sagas: the owner began negotiations
in 1975, the repairs were finished in 1983. Interior scaffolding placed
by the Department of the Environment, supports the medieval frame
at Widdington, Essex, 1980, suggesting the complexity of using
modern methods on old fabric.*

SOUTH OCKENDON, Essex. Late aisled.

STURRY, Kent. Big 16C, brick. *160*

TEMPLE CRESSING, Essex. Wheat and barley barns, magnificent medieval pair; Cecil Hewett dates Wheat Barn (140 ft long) late 13C, Barley Barn pre 1130. *See* Medieval Section. *12, 13, 62, 111, 115*

TOY'S HILL, Kent. Outridge Farm, square oasts, National Trust.

WEELEY, Essex. Gutteridge Hall, late aisled.

WENDENS AMBO, Essex. Huge, 3-porch, medieval. *160* and front jacket.

WESTENHANGER, Kent. Great medieval, hammer-beam roof. Large L-shaped plan, mostly 15C. *See* illustration in Medieval Section. *124*

WEST MALLING, Kent. Large 15C tithe barn, now serving as a chapel for an enclosed contemplative Benedictine order. Beautifully converted ten years ago by architect Robert Maguire.

WICKEN BONHUNT, Essex. Half-timbered, stylish conversion of exterior; sloping site in middle of village.

WIDDINGTON, Essex. Saga of restoration took twenty-five years, now complete. One of finest medieval barns open to public. *111–12, 161*

WITHAM, Essex. Powers Hall Farm, one of finest medieval barns, *c.*1400. Unspoilt, remote, still in use. *See* Medieval Section.

Studies in texture
Humberside, Lincolnshire, Cambridgeshire, Norfolk and Suffolk

Though the two counties are similar, generally Norfolk's agriculture was richer than Suffolk's. In Norfolk a sparser and more sandy territory was none the less the home of large estates, the barns tending to be fewer and bigger than in Suffolk, more often made of flint or brick than timber. They were built of warm red brick until the mid-eighteenth century, then with bricks of the creamy-yellow colour especially associated with railway stations and buildings, and with the big nineteenth-century maltings. There are interesting Dutch-influence crow-stepped gables.

Cambridgeshire and Lincolnshire fen barns tend to be as flat as the land around them. There are exceptions, but the agriculture must on the whole have been too poor to support big buildings.

ASHFIELD, near Stowmarket, Suffolk. At Upham House. Now antique shop belonging to Anne Marie Ponsonby.

BLOMFIELD, Norfolk. Crow-stepped gables.

BRIDGHAM, Suffolk. Gothic revival decorations *c.*1830 on façade of old barn which transform it into a smart 'folly' facing Manor Farm House.

CLEY, Norfolk. Old Hall Barn.

COPDOCK, near Ipswich, Suffolk. Crow-stepped gables, ten bays. 16C. Patterning. *42*

DERSINGHAM, Norfolk. Crow-stepped gables. Datestone 1671. Given by H.M. the Queen to Norfolk County Council who use it to store historic building materials. Patterning. *163*

EAST BERGHOLT, Suffolk. Good conversion of large thatched timber barn. Drawing room 44 × 23 ft. Frontage on River Stour at Flatford, 2 miles from the A12. Also Flatford Mill *c.*1740, where Constable was born in 1776. Splendid granary and group of mill buildings including Valley Farm *c.*1370 with big central hall and original roof timbers.

ELMSETT, Suffolk. Tithe saga, see page 11.

ELY, Cambridgeshire. King's School barn, now the school dining hall. Another big barn was demolished in 1836.

ERPINGHAM, Norfolk. Craft centre in barn at Alby. Intelligent reuse.

FAKENHAM MAGNA, Suffolk. Hall Farm Barn, flint, with 'eren', the local name for yard.

FARNHAM, near Saxmundham, Suffolk. Good 1983 conversion of big brick 18C 'transept' barn, with two big porches.

FORNHAM, near Bury St Edmunds, Suffolk. Big medieval barn in village centre. Thatch replaced by asbestos in 1983 – appearance ruined.

GAYTON THORPE, Norfolk. Great Barn, over 210 ft long, handsome 18C red brick. *164*

GREAT BEALINGS, Suffolk. Solar barn. *92–5, 94–5, 100, 105*

OPPOSITE ABOVE
Tithe barn dated 1671 at Dersingham, Norfolk, given by H.M. Queen Elizabeth II to Norfolk; now used by the local authorities there as a store for historic building fragments.

OPPOSITE BELOW
15C giant at Hales, Norfolk. The crow-stepped gables may be due to the Dutch trading connections of the region.

Barns were often subdivided for many different uses. Great Barn Farm, Gayton Thorpe, Norfolk, 18C. The changing gradient of the roof slope was created when an outshot was constructed.

BELOW
Good conversion at Great Shelford, Cambridgeshire; architect Sir Leslie Martin.

GREAT SHELFORD, Cambridgeshire. Good conversion – long and low. Sir Leslie Martin's stylish home. *164*
GREAT SNORING, Norfolk. Big medieval barn, flint walls, fine roof timbers, eight-sided rectory. Same architecture as Great Barsham Manor, famous for its decorative brick patterns.
GREAT THURLOW, Suffolk. Large 18C timber threshing barn.

Messingham, Humberside. Converted 'crue' yard, 18C.

*Because of its personal character, with hammer beams, the carpenter
of this roof at Paston, Norfolk, may eventually be identified.
Builders of most barns remain anonymous.*

GREAT WAXHAM *see* Waxham.
GRESSENHALL, Norfolk. Rural Life
Museum. 39
HALES, Norfolk. Superb brickwork and timber
roof *c*.1490. *6, 89, 163*
HOLKHAM HALL, Norfolk. Great Barn of
1791. Designed by Wyatt, as part of the famous scheme
for agricultural improvements by the Coke family,
Earls of Leicester. Coke of Norfolk, the famous
'improver', used this barn to exhibit livestock when
agriculturalists visited his annual 'sheepshearings', one
of the origins of the fashion for genteel farming. 120 ft
long. 30, 76
HUNDON, near Ipswich, Suffolk. Rectangular
yard with five old barns in a complex – partly spoiled
by one new metal barn.
KINGS FOREST, near Bury St Edmunds, Suf-
folk. Two big barns.
KING'S LYNN, Norfolk. Fermoy Arts Centre,
Red Barn. Houses a great variety of arts and activities.
LEISTON ABBEY, Suffolk. *See* illustration in
Medieval Section. *113*
MESSINGHAM, near Scunthorpe, Humberside.
Chancel Farm Barn. A splendid mid-19C traditional
Lincolnshire crue yard. U-shaped group consisting of

barn, granary, dovecot, cart shed, with wall across
front. Concrete roof tiles have been used as local pantiles were not available. *165*
OXNEAD, Norfolk. 15C hall, where the Paston
letters – 'a unique record of fifteenth-century domestic
life' – were found. Home of the 1st Earl of Yarmouth,
and of some of the Paston family. It is a delicious pale
rose colour. Splendid early brick barns with rare 15C
work and some 15C embellishments.
PASTON, Norfolk. Two datestones 1581 on
barn. *69, 70, 165*
ROUNDHAM, Norfolk. Second largest thatched

barn in the county, now collapsing for lack of a local authority grant.

SNAPE, Suffolk. Perhaps oldest in Suffolk, part of Snape Abbey foundation.

SPEXHALL, near Halesworth, Suffolk. Tithe barn recorded as early as 1618. Bought in 1968 for around £1800 by Alan Middleton-Stewart, very dilapidated. Conversion finished 1980.

STONHAM PARVA, near Stowmarket, Suffolk. Tithe Barn.

STOWMARKET, Suffolk. Museum of East Anglian Life. 39

STOWUPLAND, near Stowmarket, Suffolk. Fine central position in village, exceptional in having three threshing floors.

WAXHAM, (Great Waxham) Norfolk. Stone, brick and flint patterning. *See* illustration in Medieval Section. 74, *124*

WEST ACRE, Norfolk. Medieval buttresses, 18C barn. 48, *50*

WIMPOLE HALL, Cambridgeshire. Park Farm. Big barns rethatched 1981–82 by the National Trust. Designed by Sir John Soane *c*.1820. The biggest is timber-framed with eight bays.

Bricks and patterns

Cheshire, Shropshire, Hereford and Worcester, Staffordshire, West Midlands, Warwickshire and Leicestershire

The Midlands have been a principal home of British industry since Abraham Darby first smelted iron ore using coke instead of charcoal at Coalbrookdale in 1709, Richard Arkwright built the world's first water-powered cotton mill at Cromford in Derbyshire in 1771, and since Charles Bage designed the world's first iron-framed mill at Ditherington near Shrewsbury in 1797. Brick was first used here later than on the south coast and East Anglia – in the West Midlands brick remained rare until as late as the end of the seventeenth century. Oak and sandstone held the day, and together provided materials for the chief early agricultural build-ings.

A good collection of farm architecture is the Avon-croft Museum of Buildings at Bromsgrove near Birmingham. There, one can see the ubiquitous wood frames with wattle and daub infill, sometimes later replaced with bricks in a herringbone pattern. There

are, too, several types of half-timbered exterior. The beams were sometimes left pale, sometimes blackened. Avoncroft also makes possible an interesting com-parison of brick colours, ranging from bluish-red around Southport, to the brighter colours of Warwick.

The mid-eighteenth-century granary originally at Temple Broughton Farm, 7 miles from Avoncroft, has beautiful grain bins upstairs, and two kennels beneath the steps in which rat-catching dogs were probably kept. Three of the ten brick piers, filled with rubble, were brought intact to Avoncroft encased in splints. The renewed farm buildings at Avoncroft exhibit and catalogue interesting details. What they cannot reproduce is the romance created by centuries of use on the farm: they are too clean.

The barn at Avoncroft very drastically restored, comes from Cholstrey Court Farm at Leominster where it was built probably in the early seventeenth century. Although so late, it has cruck frames – three bays formed by four pairs of blades, unusually made of poplar, extending to the roof ridge. The big doors are made of hand-sawn elm, while the main frame is of oak.

Kenilworth in Warwickshire, has the most ornate half-timbered barn in the area – it is more than a barn, but less than a house or hall. It was built in the outer court of Kenilworth Castle in about 1570, by Elizabeth I's handsome favourite, Robert Dudley, Earl of Leicester. Ogee arch braces support the vertical posts of the timber frame, but they do more than that: with cusps on the upper and the lower sides, they give a sort of double scroll effect, a foretaste of the rocaille scrolls of two centuries later which were altogether too sophisticated ever to impinge on the barn. Tudor aristocrats liked to be flamboyant, and Leicester's bright barn, with its original handmade brick-nogging infills may seem to express some of his own swashbuck-ling character.

Shugborough Park Farm in Staffordshire was built by Lord Anson, a pioneer of the new agriculture in *c*.1800. The neo-Grecian monuments in the main gardens to the house were designed in the 1760s by James Stuart, but much of the house and most of the farm buildings were redesigned and remodelled by Samuel Wyatt – the farm buildings being completed by 1805. There is an agricultural museum in the stable wing; here too is the J. E. C. Peters' archive of photo-graphs and statistics of south Staffordshire barns. Since 1976 the Friends of Shugborough Park Farm have been breeding the old local types of livestock and exhibiting them to the public. One of the barns in the ornamental Georgian group housed the earliest fully mechanical threshing machine – the barn's clean brick and tilework is good enough for the finest country villa. Shugborough, more than anywhere, suggests the excitement of the Agricultural Revolution with improvement in productivity, stimulated by artistocratic patronage.

This reconstructed wattle may originally have been covered with some sort of mud nogging. Avoncroft Museum, Bromsgrove, Hereford and Worcester.

BELOW
White Barn Farm, Shugborough, Staffordshire, part of Lord Anson's model farm, 18C. The central building housed Britain's first stationary threshing machine.

ACTON SCOTT, near Church Stretton, Shropshire. Working farm museum. Unremarkable barns
still in use. 34

ALKINGTON, Shropshire. Datestone 1793 on
elegant brick barn. *48, 74, 132–3*

ALVANLEY, near Runcorn, Cheshire. Datestones 1582, 1871, on adjoining barns in impressive
group. *74, 75, 168*

ASTON MUNSLOW, Shropshire. The White
House Country Life Museum. 39

AVONCROFT *see* Bromsgrove

BIRMINGHAM, West Midlands. Blakesley Hall,
City Museum's Elizabethan farmhouse with barn.

BREDON, near Tewksbury, Hereford and Worcester. National Trust, 14C, burned out in 1980. Local
limestone walls and most old oak timbers survived.

BELOW
*Alvanley, Cheshire. Dated 1582, unusually late for the Gothic
style.*

Newly restored for approx. £100,000. 134 × 44 ft. *See illustrations in Medieval Section.* 110, *118–19*, 137

BRINSOP, Hereford and Worcester. Fine medieval manor.

BROMSGROVE, Hereford and Worcester. Avoncroft Museum of Buildings. 36, 166, *167*

CAREY, near Ross-on-Wye, Hereford and Worcester. Good conversion on isolated site. *168–9*

CHEYNE LONGVILLE, Shropshire. Forlorn in field, stone medieval Palace Barn, once belonged to the Bishop of Hereford.

COALBROOKDALE, Telford, Shropshire. Long Warehouse. Part of what is now a very big complex of displays illustrating early iron and Industrial Revolution equipment. The Sir Arthur Elton collection of agricultural and industrial history housed here

LEFT AND BELOW
Bold and confident conversion on isolated site. Carey, near Ross-on-Wye, Hereford and Worcester.

Typical of the Welsh border; half-timbering at Dilwyn, Hereford and Worcester. Barn converted into apartment flats.

RIGHT
Superb 15C half-timbering with arch braces; a great barn is above the gateway. Mavesyn Ridware, Staffordshire.

was opened in 1983, converted at a cost of £175,000 by Telford Development Corporation, from the original 1870s colonnaded warehouse, only yards from the furnace where in 1709 ironmaster Abraham Darby first smelted iron, using coke as fuel, so furthering the progress of the Industrial Revolution.

COLWALL, Hereford and Worcester. 14C roof.

DILWYN, Hereford and Worcester. Half-timbering black and white. *170*

DUNHAM MASSEY PARK, Cheshire (National Trust). Old mill of 1616, originally for corn, has perhaps the only surviving tree-cutting frame saw still working.

ECCLESTON, Cheshire. Model farm for Duke of Westminster's Grosvenor Estate 1870–75.

HEIGHTLEY, near Chirbury, Shropshire. Ten-bay, medieval, with cusped wind-braces.

HODNET, Shropshire. Box frame, brick nogging. 20, *21*, 42, *43*

KENILWORTH, Warwickshire. Earl of Leicester's barn. 42, 166

KINTON, Shropshire. Barn and cottage planning threats.

KINWARTON, Hereford and Worcester (near Alcester). 14C dovecot with ogee doorway.

LEDBURY, Hereford and Worcester. 14C roof.

LEIGH, Hereford and Worcester. Leigh Court. Big early 14C cruck-framed barn, slowly decaying. *42, 46, 114, 115*

LLANGARRON, Hereford and Worcester. Heavy red group. *18, 19, 73*

MARTLEY, Hereford and Worcester. Black and white half-timbering.

MATHON, Hereford and Worcester. 14C roof.

MAVESYN RIDWARE, near Lichfield, Staffordshire. Great hall/barn over 15C gateway. *49, 170–1*

MIDDLE LITTLETON, Hereford and Worcester. 13C, great timbers. *See* illustration in Medieval Section. *59, 110, 130, 137, 192*

NETHER ALDERLEY, Cheshire. National Trust. Corn mill of 1580. Remarkable oak timber post and truss: dated interior.

NORTHWICH, Cheshire. Arley Court Barn. Cruck-framed museum tea-rooms.

NUPEND, near Cradley, Hereford and Worcester. North of the A4103 towards Suckley. Great tithe barn used as an antique and exhibition gallery.

OAKHAM, Leicestershire. Rutland County Museum, Camose Street. *39*

PENRHOS COURT, Hereford and Worcester. Two barns used as restaurant and brewery.

PIRTON, Hereford and Worcester. Cruck frame. *47*

SHUGBOROUGH, Staffordshire. Lord Anson's model farm. *31, 32, 76, 166, 167*

STOKE PRIOR, Leominster, Hereford and Worcester, Wickton Court Farm. Barn complex conversion.

STYAL, near Altrincham, Cheshire. Quarry Bank

Mill of 1784 – a growing museum of the early cotton industry. Early conversions by the founder, Samuel Greg, of several barns at Farm Fold, Shaw's Fold and Oak Farm. Methodist chapel adapted from a barn in 1837.

WELLINGBOROUGH, Hereford and Worcester. Tithe barn, converted by local authority.

WEOBLEY, Hereford and Worcester. Black and white half-timbered.

WICK, near Pershore, Hereford and Worcester. Good conversion of brick and half-timbered block, possibly 18C. In the village centre, it was owned by jeweller Marilynn Nicholson. Interior spectacular, includes cast iron spiral staircase and old fireplaces.

Grey stone in Wales and the North

Wales, Merseyside, Lancashire, Cumbria, Nottinghamshire, Derbyshire, Greater Manchester, Yorkshire, Durham, Northumberland, Cleveland and Tyne and Wear

Further west into Wales, the soil was often, as in Scotland, too poor to support agriculture, and therefore to earn many barns. There are, however some good examples.

One of the finest barns in Wales, and it is no giant, is Monk's Barn in Abergavenny. In West Glamorgan, the Gower Farm Trail, set up by the County Council and the Countryside Commission, includes several stone barns with huge stone porches.

Old habits endure. In Powys, for example, cruck barns with the ridge beams supported by curved crucks rising from floor level, were still being built well into the eighteenth century. Elsewhere in Britain, the cruck frame had gone out of use two centuries earlier. Happily the property developers are unlikely to reach these stone barns of Wales for some time to come: the population of Welsh farmlands is too thin to need much new building.

In Cumbria and the Lake District the barns are built with slate roofs, often using Tilberthwaite slate, and walls are made of slabs of Coniston stone. Across the hills in the Yorkshire Dales, the barns are more numerous, sometimes several in one field, but they are smaller and poorer, and made of grey magnesium limestone blocks with stone roof slates, the whole giving a colour that is grey or dark brown as opposed to Lakeland's barns of black or purple.

Throughout the North of England, the barns were mostly too small to be used for threshing: they were built to keep animals warm in winter, and to dry hay and store crops in summer. Here the prominent southern features are absent – those generous side gables to shelter the threshers and the loaded wagon, and the

Spinning galleries for weaving, before the development of the mills. 'Kendal cloth' was mentioned by Shakespeare and was well known. Boon Crag, Cumbria.

hips at the end of the roof gables to make thatching weatherproof to the edge of the roof.

Agricultural enlightenment came late to the north-west. Elsewhere improvements in farming technique depended on the patronage and wealth of the aristocrats, who were rare in this area. Celia Fiennes, diarist and traveller, at the end of the seventeenth century recorded, '. . . sad little huts made up of dry walls and stones piled together'.

The bank barn is an ingenious local invention. Built along a slope, it allowed cattle, horses and sheep into the lower level from one side, which opened onto a farmyard which would receive the dung, provide water and an area for exercise. This lower floor might be divided into a cowshed at one end, a horse stable the other, with a cart-shed in the middle. From the other side, at the higher level, large doors would give access to the fields. There might be a threshing floor inside; often too, there would be outshots or outshuts both above and below, providing extra storage space. Hay and fodder could be tossed from the upper level into the yard below to feed the animals, or straight

*Typical Lakeland, Coniston stone walls, Tilburthwaite slate roof.
'Through' stones penetrating walls to help bind the small stones
together. Two similar 18C barns near Buckden, North Yorkshire.*

down through trap doors; the heat rising from the
animals would help warm and dry the hay. The ship-
pens or byres, just high enough for the animals to stand,
might border the yard. A good example of a barn like
this is dated 1879 at High Brundrigg Farm just east
of Kendal in Cumbria. Townend Barn at Troutbeck
near Ambleside with a datestone of 1666, but possiby
eighteenth-century, is more ambitious with two large
wings and a canopy, built on a steeper site. It belongs
to the National Trust. It has a lakeland spinning

gallery, or covered wooden arcade; another is at Yew Tree Farm, Kendal.

The enclosure of the common land probably led to more efficient agriculture; the commons pasture would no longer be overused, livestock would be less prone to disease. But the resulting bigger farms encountered a communications problem when they occurred in hilly country. This problem was solved by the building of small stone field barns, which are such a feature of the Yorkshire countryside in particu/ lar; they were built mainly for storing hay. Often, these barns were built on a slope like the bigger bank barns; calves would be tethered in the lower level. The cattle were brought to the field barn to feed on the hay and they would also manure the field around it. The farmer constantly walked or rode from barn to barn with water and food. Sometimes a half/floor would allow hay to be thrown into the lower stall. In Yorkshire, the field or hog barn was usually a very humble one/room affair with no intermediate floor, sometimes not even a rudimentary manger.

Bigger farms also meant that more produce was stored in the central farmstead, in a larger main barn, sometimes joined to the farmhouse itself and called a laithe house or long house. It may have been that grow/ ing prosperity in the eighteenth century enabled the farmer to built a new barn onto the end of his old home. But there was no dramatic or sudden modernization of buildings

Maulds Meaburn is a typically remote Cumbrian village. It has datestones on its barns of 1708, 1753, 1780 and 1799. Of the thirty/six stone farm buildings, twenty/nine are barns. It is no exaggeration to claim that most of the buildings in the majority of the isolated northern villages are barns. The problem of the north now is, simply, that too many barns are falling down and there are too few people to use them.

These small stone barns in the Dales not only have an intimate style of their own, their existence has also produced a vocabulary. The small barn for sheep was a *hoghouse*, hence the name hog barn now used for all dale field barns; the home for calves was a *calf hull*. The cowshed, called a *laith* or *lathe*, is also sometimes a *shippen*, *mistal* or *byre*. Haystacks were called *lumps* or *stamps*.

Vertical spars were often used in the roof instead of the usual horizontal lath, to provide the foundation for thatch made of ling, the local type of heather. The floors are beautifully contrived, better than in the dry south; cobbles where the animals stand are called *stand/*

ABOVE
Lakeland's most ambitious bank barn, built on the steep slope behind Coniston Old Hall, Cumbria. National Trust.

OPPOSITE ABOVE
Into Wales the stone layers become thinner; here there is an original cider press beneath the arches, a granary above, a barn beside. Crowfield, near Abergavenny, Gwent.

OPPOSITE BELOW
Typical Merseyside: Flat arches, rough stone finish. Daub Lane, near Rufford, Lancashire.

ings or *booses*. Large stones provide an edging to the area raised up for animals, and are called *settlestones*. *Boskins* of stone or oak are the partition divisions into which animals are tethered, often wide enough for a pair of animals in each.

Lofts were made with birch sticks covered with sods, to form a floor above the main tie beams. The space for hay was a *sink mew*. Cows were fastened to a ring on the upright pole – the *ridstake* or *rudster* – by a loop and toggle or *clog*. The milking stool in the barn was a *coppy*. The main floor was a *group*. A ladder was a *stee*, a muck fork was a *cowl rake* or *gripe*, the area it cleaned was a *mew* or a *mewstead*.

By 1794 Tuke, in his *General Views of Agriculture*, was writing of horses as a large part of farmers' stock. By 1837 William Howitt in Dent, in Cumbria, referred to dun horses as 'highly prized for drawing in ladies' pony carriages'. Farm life became more mobile, primitive sledges were replaced by wheeled carts, private enclosures succeeded the common pasture behind every village in the dales.

The new eighteenth-century prosperity is reflected in big new barns like Whernside Manor Farm Barn, in Dentdale, built about 1750 by the Sill family from riches earned from Jamaican sugar and in Liverpool shipping. But the broadening horizons of international industry and trade, while enriching the country with some fine buildings like Coniston Old Hall and Whernside Manor, impoverished it more by sucking its population into the big cities. In one mile of Swaledale alone there are six hundred small hog barns

and they represent a past that has truly vanished. Their only use in the future is for camping or for conversion to private homes.

Two majestic ruins in the far north are reminders of the antiquity of many barns; in North Yorkshire, near Northallerton, is Mount Grace Priory, the best example of a Carthusian monastery in the country. It is an ideal place to study a big Charterhouse and its accompanying farm and barn foundations which are now owned by the National Trust.

Further north still, in Northumberland at Tynemouth, is a Benedictine Priory, founded in *c.*627, whose present buildings date from around 1100. Foundations have survived there of no less than three barns close to the church. They may have been the oldest barn buildings in the north – evidence of the wealth of the early abbeys there.

In Northumberland, larger barns with stone arcades

are a feature of the coastal strip, for example at Beal on the mainland by Lindisfarne Island. They are cart-sheds, shelters from wind and rain, and barns combined.

A northern barn still worked in the old way, with telling architectural details, including owl hole. Oxenhope Farm, Hebden Bridge, North Yorkshire. c.1780

A handsome lowland group of big barns can be seen at Catholes on the road from Dent to Oxenholme in Cumbria; it makes an interesting comparison with the highland settlement in Yorkshire, at Camhouses. Here the small barns clustered by their remote farm-house, are now the nucleus of a new Yorkshire Dales National Park camping and barn enterprise, in miles of beautiful, unspoiled hills.

ABERGAVENNY, Gwent. Monks' Barn. 172
BAMPTON, Cumbria. Crowstep gables with 18C knobs.
BANKS, near Brampton, Cumbria. Museum for local crafts in farmhouse and barn near Lanercost Priory.
BARDEN, North Yorkshire. Cruck frames nearby.
BEAL, Northumberland. Good stone farm group. 179
BEAMISH, near Stanley, County Durham. Beamish Hall, North of England Open Air Museum. 18C. Home Farm shows agricultural history. 39
BILLINGTON, Lancashire. Hacking Hall, good cruck-framed interior, new exterior.
BLACKROD, near Bolton, Greater Manchester. Barn Acre a good conversion of c.18C stone barn and brick outbuildings into six dwellings. Architect Malcolm Cundick.
BOLTON ABBEY, North Yorkshire. Big, aisled, medieval origins, 18C outside. 42, 45, 115
BOON CRAG, Cumbria. Spinning gallery. 'Kendal cloth' made from Lakeland sheeps' wool was mentioned by Shakespeare. 172-3
BROADGATE, Broughton-in-Furness, Cumbria. Large stone barn with canopy for shelter round the ground floor.
BUCKDEN, North Yorkshire. 'Through' stones – big stones penetrating wall both through and sideways to bind the small stones together. Two typical 18C barns. 174-5
CALDEBECK, near Wigtown, Cumbria. Good conversion belonging to Dr Michael Cox.
CAMHOUSES, North Yorkshire. Camping barn. One of the best sites in Europe on top of the moors. Very isolated. 104-5, 180
CARDIFF, South Glamorgan. St Fagans Castle Folk Museum. Barn, farm group from Maentwrog. 39
CARLISLE, Cumbria. See illustration in Medieval Section. 11
CATHOLES, near Oxenholme, Cumbria.

Camping barn. Too many new installations for visual comfort. Daily fee for visitors. 180
CLIBURN, near Penrith, Cumbria. Arts centre barn.
CONISTON, Cumbria. Great hall. Fine lakeland chimneys. Datestones 1630 and 1760. Old Hall Barn, 18C. Lakeland's most ambitious bank barn. 72-3, 176
CROWFIELD, near Abergavenny, Gwent. Typical multi-purpose barn/cider press/granary. 177
DAUB LANE, near Rufford, Lancashire. Typical Merseyside flattened arches. 177
DENTDALE, North Yorkshire. Whernside Manor Farm Barn, big 18C. 176
EARL STANFIELD, Derbyshire. Handsome stone farm group.
EAST RIDDLESDEN, near Keighley, West Yorkshire. Medieval, stone, aisled. See illustration in Medieval Section. 13, 60, 115
EGSTOW, Derbyshire. Interesting for wide-ranging historical theories. 47, 53
FARNLEY, near Otley, West Yorkshire. Turner lived and painted by good northern group, probably designed by John Carr of York c.1795. 26-7
GAWTHORPE HALL, Padiham, Lancashire. Great Barn, Grade I, stone, 1604. After planning discussions supported by SPAB, it is now an activities centre. Bought by the National Trust to complete the rest of the estate which they had been given.
GLENCOYNE, Potterdale, Cumbria. A statesman's farm – good group. Farmhouse and barn-cum-cow-byre or shippon, are joined in typical long house fashion; 1629 datestone on house.
GOWER, West Glamorgan. Farm Trail. 172, 181
GRASSINGTON, North Yorkshire. Shaped 'kneelers' on lower ends of gables. John Wesley preached here. Probably related to Grassington Old Hall, built partly in 13C. 19
GREETLAND, near Halifax, West Yorkshire. Clay House Barn. Late 16C, owned by Calderdale Council. On 1 June 1980, the Observer newspaper published a photograph, showing it in state of decay, with a plea for support – 1500 replies were received and the barn is now being restored.
HALIFAX, West Yorkshire. West Yorkshire Folk Museum at Shibden Hall. 39
HEBDEN BRIDGE, North Yorkshire. Oxenhope Farm, 18C barn, 1869 farmhouse in same idiom. Traditional styles live on. 178-9
HEMMEL, Northumberland. Open-fronted shelter

Unusually large for the Lakes : Troutbeck barn, opposite Townend House, Cumbria. National Trust.

for animals. The Duke of Northumberland built many similar farms in the 1830s around Alnwick.

HIGH BRUNDRIGG, near Kendal, Cumbria. Datestone 1879. *74, 174*

HUTTON-LE-HOLE, North Yorkshire. Ryedale Folk Museum. *39*

KELDWICK, near Thornwaite, North Yorkshire. Good conversion of old Yorkshire stone barn. *98, 99, 100*

KELHAM ISLAND, Sheffield, South Yorkshire. New industrial museum showing traditional Sheffield craftsmen's 'Little Mesters'' (masters') workshops.

KENDAL, Cumbria. Yew Tree Farm has spinning gallery. *69, 175*

KILNSEY, North Yorkshire. Medieval field barns. *18, 69, 70–1*

LEATHLEY, North Yorkshire. One of the grander Wharfedale barns.

LINTON-IN-CRAVEN, North Yorkshire. Long, medieval. Several entrances each side, multi-purpose.

LLANDEWI, West Glamorgan. Llandewi Castle Farm just west of Knelston. Part of West Glamorgan County Council's Gower Farm Trail. Camping site by barn which has huge hipped gable porch whose roof is level with main roof ridge.

MARSKE, North Yorkshire. Gothic revival barn *c.*1780, perhaps designed by John Carr of York.

MATHAFARN, Machynlleth, Powys. Slotted openings.

MATHRAFAL, Powys. Dutch barn with slits and columns.

MEIFOD, Powys. Good brick-built granary. Meifod valley has several good brick-nogged barns.

METHLEY, West Yorkshire, 7 miles southeast of Leeds. Tithe barn.

MOUNT GRACE PRIORY *see* Northallerton.

NEWTON, Northumberland. Hunday National Tractor and Farm Museum. 38

NORTHALLERTON, North Yorkshire. Mount Grace Priory. Best Carthusian monastery in Britain. 178

OXNOP, North Yorkshire. In Swaledale, 2 miles southeast of Muker. Laithe house. No internal connection between sections.

RONDUAR, Powys. Cruck frames.

ROTHERHAM, South Yorkshire. Whiston Hall Long Barn, one of the oldest in the area.

ST DONATS, South Glamorgan. Arts Centre. Tithe barn used for concerts and theatre.

ST FAGANS *see* Cardiff.

SLEDMERE, Humberside. Fine, large pitching hole at top of gable.

SWALEDALE, North Yorkshire. Small 'hog' or field barns decaying by the hundred; *see also* Marske, Oxnop.

TALIARIS, Dyfed. 4 miles north of Llandilo. Occasional concerts.

TROUTBECK, Cumbria. Townend, datestone 1666, National Trust. 174, *181*

TYNEMOUTH, Northumberland. Benedictine barns.

WALLINGTON, Northumberland. At Duke Head Farm, *c.*1840. Good flattened arch arcades.

WELBECK ABBEY, Nottinghamshire. Dutch barn. 22

WHISTON, South Yorkshire. Long barn to be a Museum of Rural Life. 36

WRESSLE, near Selby, Humberside. Castle Farm Barn, 120 ft long. Rebuilt in 18C using medieval timbers.

Border surprises
Scotland

Rain – frequent in northern areas of Britain – is an enemy of barns, for wet crops cannot easily be stored; subsistence agriculture – predominant in many parts of Scotland in the past – is another threat, producing too little food for storage. It is perhaps strange, therefore, to find any barns at all in Scotland, especially as the country was subdivided into small clan holdings and torn by strife. Indeed, it was not until peace was established in the eighteenth century that a few barns were

Typical outlying small Lowlands barn. Balcarres, Fife.

OPPOSITE ABOVE
Mill, barn and farmhouse at Lothallen, near Balcarres, Fife. To the west, in the Carse of Stirling, there were many mills, similar but with round horse-gin engine houses.

OPPOSITE BELOW
Typical of Scottish Lowlands: crisp 18C outline. The new barn here is comparatively harmonious. Balniel, Colinsburgh, Fife.

built, and then only in the fertile strips away from the mountains. The nineteenth-century depopulation of the Highlands and the invasion of the grouse moors by the rich gentry from the south had little effect on these farms which still struggled against the vagaries of the weather and the distance of the consumer.

There are, however, some elegant surprises. At Kilchiaran, on the Isle of Islay, is a semi-circular Georgian grey-stone barn complex. A circular barn is indeed a rarity. In the area around the Solway Firth are many fine farm settlements each with its own small barn. To the southwest, in Dumfries and Galloway, red sandstone is common. The most romantic barn ruins are at Sweetheart Abbey, near New Abbey, founded in 1273 by Devorguila, Lady of Galloway, wife of John Balliol of Barnard Castle, one of the regents of Scotland. She kept her husband's embalmed heart after his death and founded the abbey in his memory.

One area of good free-standing grey-stone farm

Clear Scottish 18C detailing, Balniel, Colinsburgh, Fife.

Crow-stepped gables at Fala, south-east of Edinburgh, Lothian.

barns is near Stirling in Central Region: they are small, unpretentious and effective. Another group is in the rich valley of Glen Devon, Tayside. In Fife and to the north, brick mingles with the stone: the sixteenth-century Preston Mill, 5 miles west of Dunbar in Lothian, is the oldest working water-driven wheat mill in Scotland, retiring from use only in 1957. Its conical kiln and red pantiles are a little reminiscent of a Kentish oasthouse and barn, as is its neighbouring Phantassie Doocot (dovecot) which had room for five hundred birds. Boath Doocot, 2 miles east of Nairn, is a seventeenth-century complex of farming prosperity. At Drumeldrie near Colinsburgh in Fife, there is a classy octagonal, tiled, brick outshot for a horse and rotating engine, built on to the red-tiled barn. Lothallen Mill near Balcarres in Fife is one of the most handsome groups in Scotland; the mill dates from about 1800 with a millstone inside inscribed 1612, while the barns seem late eighteenth-century. Balniel Barn nearby is of similar distinction with huge grey-stone quoins and black shiny infills almost like knapped flint in their luminosity.

At Flatfield near Errol, in Tayside, the farmhouse is dated 1785. Its barn is a good specimen of clay building, popular in the north of Scotland before cheap stone became available in the nineteenth century. This structure, built on a stone plinth, may be unique. The solid clay walls are penetrated by floor joists from the interior; every third joist is pegged outside the wall against a timber plate. On one side, short timbers are stapled to the ends of these joists, and joined in pairs for added security. The Angus Folk Museum in Glamis on Tayside, housed in seventeenth-century cottages, now forms a typical farm settlement. It shows well the life inside these small farmsteads.

Poverty was the normal rule in this region, and poverty bred its own vocabulary here as in Yorkshire: for the pre-stone buildings made of a sort of osier-hurdle skeleton, one denomination was 'stake and rice'. It was also dignified with such variations as 'stab and rice', 'claut and clay', 'stud and mud', 'clam staff and daub', 'daub and stower', 'rice and stower', 'riddle and daub', 'strae and rake', 'rod and daub', 'split and daub', 'cat and clay', 'clay and mott', 'clay and wattle'.

Heather or straw rope instead of osier would be called 'stake and tow' or 'stab and tow'. All of this suggests that while we have become more prosperous with our mechanized intensive farming, we are losing not only Britain's barns but also a whole world of words.

AUCHINDRAIN, near Inveraray, Strathclyde. Museum of Country Life. 36

BALCARRES, Fife. Handsome 18C barns. Also Lothallen Mill. *182, 183, 185*

BALNIEL, near Colinsburgh, Fife. Small 18C, unusually fine brick and stone work. *183, 184, 185*

DRUMELDRIE, near Colinsburgh, Fife. Horse gin, octagonal, tile and brick. 185

DUNBAR, Lothian. Preston Mill, working water mill. Nearby Phantassie doocot (dovecot). National Trust for Scotland. 185

FALA, Lothian. Crowstepped gables are most common in Scotland and East Anglia. Some construction here is 19C though 17C in style. *185*

FLATFIELD, near Errol, Tayside. Farmhouse 1785, clay barn, possibly unique structure. 185

GAITGIL, near Twynholm, Dumfries and Galloway. Steading (farm settlement with barn) converted to house and pottery.

GARLIESTON, Dumfries and Galloway. Penkiln Farm – good steadings conversion.

GLADSMUIR, Greendyke, Lothian. Fine model farm steading, 1832, with crow-stepped gables, doocot, straw barn.

GLAMIS, Tayside. Angus Folk Museum. 36, 185

GLEN DEVON, Tayside. Grey stone barns.

GLENLEE, Dumfries and Galloway. Steading converted to four dwellings.

KILCHIARAN, Strathclyde. On the Isle of Islay, semi-circular. 182

NAIRN, Highland. 17C Boath Doocot (dovecot). National Trust for Scotland. 185

ST BOSWELLS, Roxburgh, Borders. Model 18C farm and barns. *186*

STIRLING, Central. Good small barns, many circular horse gins for mills.

Model farm in Scotland c.1800. Village, farm buildings, barns – all built together so they are aesthetically pleasing as well as functionally convenient. St Boswells, Roxburgh, Borders.

Glossary

ASHLAR masonry with even face and square edges.

BANK BARN usually small barn built on slope, with two storeys at one end and only one at the other.

BAY space formed by vertical posts, buttresses or roof beams along a barn interior.

BOX FRAME skeleton grid frame, usually wood, with soft in-fills, wattle and daub, or brick nogging. Distinct from cruck frame and from post-and-truss construction.

BRACE subsidiary timber strengthener; wind brace in plane of roof; sling brace between wall post and roof rafter.

BRICK NOGGING brickwork between wood load-bearing frame.

BYRE cowshed.

COB clay mixed with gravel and straw into lumps, used for building walls especially in Devon.

COLLAR horizontal beam joining the two sides of the roof. Runs between and ties together the sloping rafters, parallel to the main tie beam.

CORBEL projecting stone or piece of timber, usually to support a weight above; sometimes a purely decorative survival from an early function.

CRUCK timber beams, usually curved, sloping inwards and joined at the top, to form a vertical load-bearing frame.

DRESSINGS stone or brick, worked to a decorative finish.

FIELD HOUSE, FIELD BARN, HOG BARN Yorkshire terms used to describe the small stone barns in the Dales and moors, often one barn in each stone-walled field.

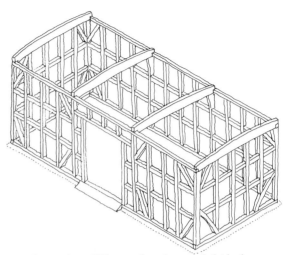

Box frame. The in-fill between the timbers may be brick, clay or wattle and often makes a beautiful decorative effect outside

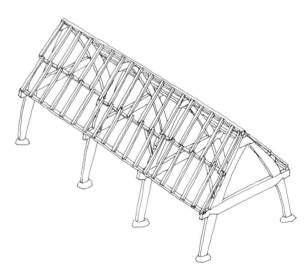

Cruck frame showing bays formed inside by the pairs of cruckblades

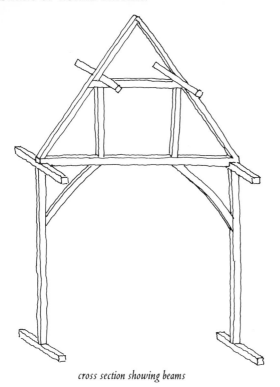

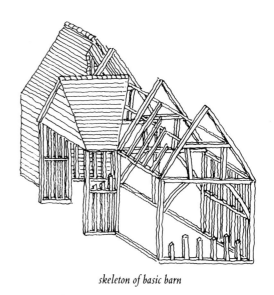

A typical barn with cross-section showing beams. The way they are fitted together varies according to date and place

cross section showing beams

skeleton of basic barn

Some typical barn shapes and details

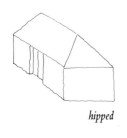

hipped

gabled

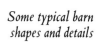

half-hipped

barn with lofted stable

barn with cattle aisles

small stable with pitching hole to loft

gabled porch

hipped porch

canopy with cheeks

hipped canopy

FLAIL tool for threshing made of a wooden staff, and stouter end called a swingle or swipple, the two connected often by eel skin.

GABLE the wall at the end of a ridged roof, generally triangular, sometimes surmounted with 'crow steps' or with decorative finials on top.

GAMBREL *see* mansard

HIPPED ROOF with sloped instead of vertical ends.

HOG BARN *see* field house.

LAITHE, LAITHE HOUSE farmhouse and barn combined, usually with no inter-communication inside. Built in the Pennines and Peak District, mostly rather late, *c.*1800.

LINHAY open hay loft above cattle shed.

LINTEL horizontal beam or stone, bridging an opening such as a window or door.

LONG HOUSE farmhouse and barn or shippon combined, usually with cross passage inside. The normal substitute for a barn in Devon, around Dartmoor, also found in Cumbria and north-east Yorkshire. Seldom built after 17C.

MANSARD characteristic roof form with slope of two pitches instead of the more normal one. Also called *gambrel* from the shape of a horse's ankle and knee.

MIDSTREY door or porch.

OUTSHUT, OUTSHOT lean-to structure or shed built onto the main barn.

OWL HOLE *see* drawings.

PANTILE roofing tile curved to an ogee shape, one curve much larger than the other. Used normally to describe traditional red Norfolk tiling.

PLINTH projecting base of a wall or column.

POST AND TRUSS scheme of building where the roof load is borne not by the wall but by internal vertical posts and horizontal trusses.

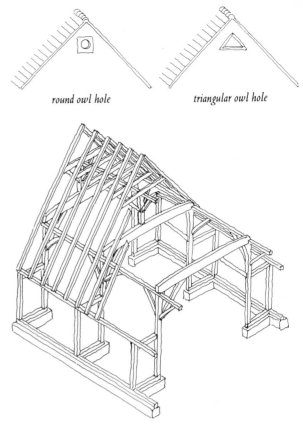

round owl hole   *triangular owl hole*

Post and truss construction. Note the aisle outside the main posts

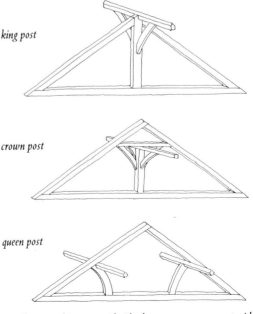

king post

crown post

queen post

Roof trusses : king post with ridge beam at top, crown post with collar at top and queen post

PURLIN horizontal beam in the plane of the roof, to support rafters. *See* drawings.

RIDGE beam along top of roof; when there is a beam along the ridge this suggests added strength and later date. *See* drawings.

ROOF TRUSSES *see* drawings.

SCANTLING carpentry measurements.

SCARF a joint of two timbers longitudinally.

SHIPPEN, SHIPPON cow, or farmhouse.

SHORE diagonal wooden buttress.

STEAD bay.

STEADING farm settlement with barn.

TIE BEAM horizontal transverse beam in a roof, tying together the feet of pairs of rafters to counteract the outward thrust caused by the weight of the roof pressing down.

TIMBER FRAME *see* box frame.

WATTLE AND DAUB an interlace of twigs, rods and branches, plastered with clay or mud. The commonest form of in-fill for a box-framed barn.

WEATHER-BOARDING usually horizontal planks nailed to the uprights of timber box-framed barns. The planks overlap and are generally wedge shaped, thicker on top. Vertical planks were used in early weather-boarding.

SPAB – The Society for the Protection of Ancient Buildings

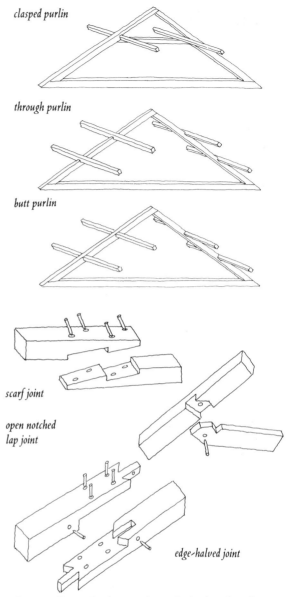

clasped purlin

through purlin

butt purlin

scarf joint

open notched lap joint

edge-halved joint

Some scarf joints. Cecil Hewett has evolved a chronological sequence of the use of these, and of more complex joints, to help to date beams from the late 12C to the late 16C

Selected bibliography

ABRAMS, LAWRENCE and KATHLEEN *Salvaging Old Barns and Houses* Blandford Press 1983

ALCOCK, N. W. *Articles in Devonshire Association Report* Devonshire 1969; *Catalogue of crucks* Vernacular Architecture Group, Phillimore; *Cruck construction – An Introduction and Catalogue* Council for British Archaeology 1982

AVONCROFT MUSEUM OF BUILDINGS *Guide Book including Cholstrey Barn c.1700* Avoncroft Museum 1974

BRUNSKILL, R. W. *Vernacular Architecture* Faber 1978; *Vernacular Architecture of the Lake Countries* Faber 1974; *Traditional Farm Buildings of Britain* Gollancz 1982

BRUNSKILL, R. W., CLIFTON-TAYLOR, A., LINSTROM, D., OPIE, M. and TRINDER, B. *Timber, iron, clay. Five essays on their use in building* Midlands 1975

CLIFTON-TAYLOR, ALEC *The Pattern of English Building* Faber 1972; with IRESON, A. S. *English Stone Building* Gollancz 1983

DARLEY, GILLIAN *National Trust Book of the Farm* National Trust/Weidenfeld & Nicholson 1981

DAVIES, N. W. I. *Barns and Barn Conversions in Cumbria* Brunel University 1979

DICKINSON, J. C. *Monastic Life in Mediaeval England* A & C Black 1961

EAST SUSSEX COUNTY PLANNING DEPARTMENT *Barn Trails, Walks in East Sussex* 1979

ESSEX COUNTY COUNCIL *The Essex Countryside Historic Barns – a planning appraisal* County Hall Chelmsford 1980

EVANS, GEORGE EWART *Ask the fellows who cut the hay* Faber and Faber 1956

FOWLER, PETER *Farms in England Prehistoric to Present* HMSO 1983

HANSFORD WORTH, R. *Dartmoor* David & Charles 1967

HARRIS, RICHARD *Traditional Farm Buildings* Arts Council Catalogue 1979

HARVEY, NIGEL *Industrial Archaeology of Farming* Batsford 1980; *Old Farm Buildings* Shire Publications 1980

HEWETT, CECIL *The Development of Carpentry* David & Charles 1969; *Essex Church Carpentry* (second edition) Phillimore; *English Historic Carpentry* Phillimore 1980

HUDSON, KENNETH *The Shell Guide to Country Museums* Heinemann 1980

HORN, W. and BORN, E. *The Barns of the Abbey of Beaulieu (Gt Coxwell, St Leonard's)* University of California, Berkeley 1965

INNOCENT, C. E. *The Development of English Building Construction* David & Charles 1916/1971

LACY, H. M. & U. E. *Timber-framed Buildings of Steyning* The Authors, Flexiprint, Worthing 1974

MASON, R. T. *Framed Buildings of England* Coach Publishing House, Horsham; *Framed Buildings of the Weald* (second edition) Mark Fitch Fund/Author 1969

MINGAY, GORDON E. *The Victorian Countryside* Routledge & Kegan Paul 1982

PEARCE, DAVID (ed.) *The Barns Book* Society for the Protection of Ancient Buildings (SPAB) 1982

PERKINS, J. W., BROOKS, A. T. and PEARCE, A. E. *Bath Stone, A Quarry History* University College Cardiff and Kingshead Press, Bath 1979

PETERS, J. E. C. *The Development of Farm Buildings in Western Lowland Staffordshire* Manchester University Press/ Fitch Charity 1969

PEVSNER, N. *Buildings of England* Penguin. Few barns mentioned; but 2 vols on Gloucestershire contain interesting comments.

REID, RICHARD *The Shell Book of Cottages* Michael Joseph 1977

REYNOLDS, JOHN *The Hampshire Barn* Architectural Association thesis 1978

ROBINSON, J. M. *Georgian Model Farms* Oxford 1984

SUDDARDS, ROGER W. *Listed Buildings: the Law and Practice* Sweet & Maxwell 1982

TAYLOR, ALAN *Buckinghamshire Barn and Barn Building Survey* Buckinghamshire County Planning Committee

VINCE, JOHN *Old farms, an illustrated guide* John Murray 1982

WADE, JANE, (ed.) *Traditional Kent Buildings* Canterbury College of Art, Kent County Council Education Committee 1980

ZEUNER, C. S. H. (ed.) *Weald and Downland Open Air Museum, Singleton* Guide and Catalogue 1977

Epilogue

First, I must thank those numerous owners of barns who maintain their buildings with love and care; they are the heroes of this book and I wish there were more of them. Second, I am grateful to the owners who have discussed their barns with me, and allowed me to photograph and examine them. Third, Alan Taylor has kindly read my text and offered me many useful comments in this relatively uncharted territory where conjecture is still as common as fact. Finally, my patient publisher David Herbert and his perceptive editor Curigwen Lewis (and, earlier on, Georgina Evans) have helped me to complete the book, despite all difficulties of defining new county boundaries and uncertain village borders, of dating hitherto undated buildings and of condensing a mass of geographical material, into a digestible summary of regional trends.

Messrs Faber and Faber have generously allowed me to quote long passages from their remarkable survey of Suffolk country life *Ask the fellows who cut the hay* by George Ewart Evans.

Big porch one side for entrance of loaded wagon, smaller the other for exit of empty wagon after discharge of threshing load. Middle Littleton, Hereford and Worcester, National Trust, 13C.

I wrote this book not just because of a life-long love of barns. It is also the result of a frustrating three-year struggle to obtain planning permission to convert our own barn into a dwelling. This battle opened my eyes to the crisis facing so many barns today.

Graham Hughes